The
Literacy Coach's
SURVIVAL
GUIDE

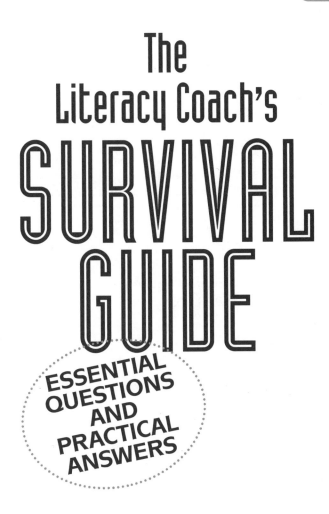

ESSENTIAL
QUESTIONS
AND
PRACTICAL
ANSWERS

CATHY A. TOLL

Toll and Associates
Normal, Illinois, USA

INTERNATIONAL
Reading Association
800 BARKSDALE ROAD, PO BOX 8139
NEWARK, DE 19714-8139, USA
www.reading.org

The International Reading Association attempts, through its publications, to provide a forum for a wide spectrum of opinions on reading. This policy permits divergent viewpoints without implying the endorsement of the Association.

Editorial Director   Matthew W. Baker
Managing Editor   Shannon T. Fortner
Permissions Editor   Janet S. Parrack
Acquisitions and Communications Coordinator   Corinne M. Mooney
Associate Editor   Charlene M. Nichols
Administrative Assistant   Michele Jester
Assistant Permissions Editor   Tyanna L. Collins
Production Department Manager   Iona Muscella
Supervisor, Electronic Publishing   Anette Schütz
Senior Electronic Publishing Specialist   R. Lynn Harrison
Electronic Publishing Specialist   Lisa M. Kochel
Proofreader   Elizabeth C. Hunt

Project Editor   Charlene M. Nichols

Cover Design   Linda Steere; photographs (from top): Comstock, Ed Broadbelt, PhotoDisc, Digital Vision, PhotoDisc, BrandX

Web addresses in this book were correct as of the publication date but may have become inactive or otherwise modified since that time. If you notice a deactivated or changed Web address, please e-mail books@reading.org with the words "Website Update" in the subject line. In your message, specify the Web link, the book title, and the page number on which the link appears.

Library of Congress Cataloging-in-Publication Data
Toll, Cathy A., 1956-
 The literacy coach's survival guide : essential questions and practical answers / Cathy A. Toll.
    p. cm.
 Includes bibliographical references and index.
 ISBN 0-87207-565-6 (alk. paper)
 1. Mentoring in education—United States. 2. Reading teachers—In-service training—United States. I. Title.
 LB1731.4.T65 2004
 428.4'071'5—dc22
Fifth Printing, January 2006   2004018814

CONTENTS

What Is This Book About?
Who Is It For?

- Why did I write this book?

- Who is the target audience for this book?

- What is in this book?

- Exactly what is a literacy coach?

- How does coaching positively affect schools, teachers, and students?

- Is there a need for coaching?

*A*few years ago, I started lifting weights, for the sake of my health and to promote weight loss. I hired a personal trainer to help me learn the basics, and she enthusiastically showed me all that I needed to know—and then some. For every muscle group, she had two or three exercises to show me. For some of the exercises, she would show me two or three options. I found myself overwhelmed and discouraged. In addition, this trainer met with me in an office that she shared with two other trainers, so we were frequently interrupted and I felt self-conscious.

I soon found a different trainer, one who taught me one set of exercises at a time. Yes, she introduced alternatives, but only when I was ready because I had learned the first set. She gave me just enough information to know the purpose of each move and how to do it safely. In addition, she came to my home, where I had no shyness about spreading out on the floor in my sweat suit and awkwardly attempting the weight lifting exercises. Four years later, I'm still using the moves the second trainer taught me, and the weight training has contributed to my loss of well over 100 pounds.

What a difference the right coach makes! As a reader of this book, you no doubt already agree with this statement and are committed to the concept of literacy coaching. I suspect that you are looking for ways to improve your own literacy coaching skills or the skills of literacy coaches with whom you work. However, I tell the story of my experience in learning to work with weights because it reminds *me* of what I need to do in this book.

By writing this book, I've become a kind of long-distance coach of coaches. I could easily be tempted to tell you much more than you want to know, overwhelming you in the process. Or I could make the information confusing to learn and remember. Or I could share the information in a "place" that wasn't very comfortable, such as by being overly academic or unclear. I, too, want to be a good coach, so I've attempted to avoid these pitfalls.

I want this book to provide literacy coaches and those who work with literacy coaches with a great deal of practical information. I work with a lot of literacy coaches, and I know that they have many questions, most of which I can assist them in answering. In addition, I want to give literacy coaches just enough background and perspective in order to coach in the most effective way. Finally, I want this book to be friendly, like a conversation. I believe the best coaching takes place in a supportive relationship. Therefore, I want my voice to come through in this book so you sense me as a person who is working alongside you, helping you to become the literacy coach you want to be.

Let's Get to Know Each Other

I come to this work as someone who has tried for 25 years to be a leader in literacy education. I have been a classroom teacher at the elementary, middle, high school, and postsecondary levels; a reading specialist; a district reading coordinator; an elementary school principal; a university faculty member; and a consultant to teachers, literacy coaches, administrators, and others. Until recently, I directed the Center for Literacy at North Central Regional Educational Laboratory (NCREL), which provides research, services, and products for educators.

I am currently the founder and lead consultant of Toll and Associates, a firm that specializes in serving literacy coaches and those who support them. Toll and Associates provides training workshops, one-to-one and small-group coaching, consultation, print resources, grant writing, research, and evaluation for literacy coaches and leaders of programs that include literacy coaching. We work with schools, school districts, and other educational organizations throughout the United States.

I've done a great deal of reading and some research on change in literacy education and on coaching in general. I'll confess, though, that most of what I believe about literacy coaching is influenced by my experiences. To be candid, I've made practically every possible mistake, both as a teacher and as a leader. However, here's the good news: I work very hard to learn from my mistakes. My practical struggles have caused me to study change and the leadership of change in graduate school and beyond. And, to my pleasant surprise, I've discovered that the insights and practices that I have developed, based upon my formal education and my education in the real world of schools, enable me to coach literacy coaches with a high degree of success.

Obviously, as an author, I can't hear the voice of you, the reader, but here's who I think you are: My hunch is that readers of this book primarily will be literacy coaches. Chances are that you are fairly new to the job because the position of literacy coach has become popular in schools only recently. You are likely to work in an elementary school or middle school setting, where the greatest number of literacy coaches is concentrated. However, you might be one of the growing group of literacy coaches who works in a secondary school setting. There also are an increasing number of you in pre-K settings because the leaders of Head Start and other early learning programs have begun to emphasize literacy coaching as a valuable model for teachers' professional development at that level. You probably taught for some years before becoming a literacy coach, but this isn't necessarily the case. And odds are that more of you are female than male, but I know that literacy coaches of both genders will be reading this book.

I'm basing these assumptions on the work that I've done with literacy coaches in the midwestern United States, the interactions I've had with literacy coaches from around the United States at conferences, and my professional reading. I know there are literacy coaches who don't fit into this profile, and I want to make them welcome here, too. Throughout the book, I use both male and female pronouns when referring to literacy coaches and to teachers and principals. I also use examples primarily from pre-K through middle school settings. I hope these choices are inclusive enough for this book's readers.

I suspect there are other readers of this book who are coaches of literacy coaches or in some other way support the work of teacher leaders. Welcome! I address literacy coaches directly in this book, but please know that I'm aware that the rest of you are out there. After all, I'm one of you. I know I would have found a book like this helpful years ago, before I figured out literacy coaching for myself, and I hope you will find it useful, too.

What Is Literacy Coaching?

Coaching is a popular term these days. Life coaches—individuals who support others in setting and meeting goals—have proliferated, especially online and on television. Business leaders are encouraged to coach employees, and references to teaching as coaching have started to appear in educational environments. Teachers who have been in the field for more than a few years probably remember the trend known as *peer coaching*, which was popular in the 1980s and early 1990s, and, in fact, a good number of educators seem to think that that's what literacy coaching is all about.

With the range and extensiveness of coaching endeavors, literacy coaches often have to clarify—for themselves and others—the nature of their work. Here is a definition of a literacy coach that I have developed:

> A literacy coach is one who helps teachers to recognize what they know and can do, assists teachers as they strengthen their ability to make more effective use of what they know and do, and supports teachers as they learn more and do more.

I'd like to point out several significant aspects of this definition. First, note that the emphasis is on teachers. As a literacy coach, your most significant clients are teachers. Student achievement is the teachers' desired outcome, and you are there to help achieve that goal, but your focus is teachers. Note, too, that this definition is written from a positive perspective; it doesn't say that the literacy coach is employed to "fix" problem situations or teachers. Another feature of the definition is that it places the literacy coach in the role of supporting teachers; in other words, the teachers are responsible for identifying their strengths and growing their capabilities, and the literacy coach is there to assist the teachers. Some literacy coaches and teachers believe that the literacy coach is there to tell the teachers what they should be doing and to make sure they do it. That is not at all the vision of literacy coaching that you'll find in this definition or in this book.

Not everyone can be a literacy coach. Literacy coaches need to be well versed in the research, theory, and practices of literacy instruction. In addition, literacy coaches need a sound understanding of teaching, learning, and child development. Literacy coaches also need knowledge of adult learning and teachers' professional development. Finally, literacy coaches need strong interpersonal skills, especially in the areas of communication and empathy, and good skills in planning and organizing. Being trustworthy, loyal, and cheerful would make a literacy coach particularly strong.

There is some overlap between the duties of a reading specialist and a literacy coach, and therefore these roles are sometimes confused. Both reading specialists and literacy coaches serve as building leaders in literacy instruction, and both support the goal of improving student achievement. However, while reading specialists focus their attention on improving student achievement by working directly with students, literacy coaches focus their attention on improving student achievement by working directly with teachers. Granted, reading specialists sometimes work directly with teachers and literacy coaches sometimes work directly with students, but these are not regular occasions. In addition, members of both groups perform additional duties, such as contributing to building-level professional development workshops and advising the principal on literacy-related matters. Given these overlapping duties, it is easy to see why confusion between reading specialists and literacy coaches may occur. To make the distinctions easier, Table 1 outlines these differences.

In some schools, reading specialists are asked to do the duties of literacy coaches as well. This makes sense, given that both roles require strong knowledge of literacy instruction. However, reading specialists often lack knowledge of the coaching processes that are essential for effective literacy coaching. In addition, the overlapping roles sometimes cause confusion among others in the school. For instance, when a reading specialist is working with a guided reading group in a teacher's classroom, it may be unclear to the teacher whether the reading specialist is demonstrating an instructional practice as a literacy coach or trying to improve the achievement of the students in the guided reading group as a reading specialist. Both goals are valuable, but the teacher will need to pay closer attention if the purpose of the guided reading lesson is to model an instructional practice.

Table 1
Comparison of Reading Specialists and Literacy Coaches

● ● ●

Reading Specialists	Literacy Coaches
Support students, parents, and administrators as well as teachers	Emphasize support for teachers, although support for others also may take place
Frequently provide direct instruction to students on a daily basis	Provide direct instruction to students primarily when demonstrating for teachers
Provide evaluations of students for a variety of reasons, including curriculum monitoring, student diagnosis, and monitoring teacher and school effectiveness	Provide evaluation of students primarily to demonstrate for teachers or to support teachers in their instructional decision making
Work directly with teachers to an extent but do not necessarily focus work on this area	Spend a great amount of time working directly with teachers in individual and small-group meetings
When working with teachers, may be responding to teachers' needs and concerns but also may be directing teachers to meet requirements or implement mandatory programs	Work with teachers mostly in response to teachers' needs and concerns

In cases where a reading specialist also is assigned literacy coaching duties, the reading specialist should work with the principal and the school staff to delineate the two roles and to make clear the focus and goals of each. In addition, the reading specialist may want to frequently remind those she works with that she plays a dual role and to explain which role she is playing in particular situations.

Why Literacy Coaching?

If you're reading this book, you've probably already decided that literacy coaching is a good idea. However, this section will provide background information on which the rest of the book will build, so it will be valuable to read even if you already believe in the effectiveness of coaching. By thinking about the purposes served by coaching, you'll have a better understanding of the recommendations I make for the coaching work you are doing.

Literacy coaching affects the school culture. Increasing evidence points to the need for school cultures to change if schools are to become better places to work and learn (Fullan & Hargreaves, 1996; Hargreaves, 1994; Sarason, 1996). A culture of collaboration and trust supports growth for the school and for the individuals involved in the school. Literacy coaching furthers such an atmosphere because coaching leads to stronger relationships and greater opportunities for educators to interact.

Literacy coaching supports significant change. Those who study school reform and teachers' professional development have found that a great deal of effort toward changing what happens in schools has not led to any significant change after all (Gibboney, 1994; Tyack & Cuban, 1995). Some of the effort simply was not effective in producing any change. However, much of the effort did make a difference—only the difference was superficial. For instance, the implementation of Individualized Education in the 1970s led to classrooms without walls but didn't change the school culture or the nature of teaching. Conversely, literacy coaching supports significant change because it provides a foundation for teacher reflection, action research, collaboration, and informed decision making, all of which can lead to significant educational changes.

Literacy coaching promotes reflection and decision making. The key to literacy coaching is that the teacher being coached does the greatest amount of work—not because literacy coaches are lazy but because they know how to encourage others to trust themselves. Literacy coaching is not about telling others what to do, but rather bringing out the best in others.

Why does this matter? Many educators believe that teaching is best when teachers are reflective (Schön, 1987; Zeichner & Liston, 1996). This makes sense, doesn't it? In order to do a job with the complexity of teaching, it is essential to be thinking about it carefully and deeply—not just about what is happening at the time but about why it happened, how it affects and is affected by other factors and events, and what it will affect in the future. For instance, if you try a new teaching strategy—for example, doing shared reading with the students—you'll do your best teaching if you think about how your use of the strategy went, including what went well, what needs improvement, what the children did well during the activity, what they tried that they hadn't tried before, and what knowledge and strategies they used during the activity. You also should look ahead and think about whether you'd use the practice again, what you'd do the same, what you'd do differently, and so on. All of this reflection would help you to make shared reading as effective as possible.

Literacy coaching assists teachers in being reflective by providing time, space, and encouragement. Time for reflection comes from one-on-one or small-group meetings in which the literacy coach and teacher(s) discuss practices, beliefs, goals, and other matters essential for consideration when doing one's best teaching. Space for reflection occurs in the interpersonal space that is created when a literacy coach and a teacher sit down for a meeting. As for encouragement, literacy coaches encourage teachers to reflect by asking them thought provoking questions, providing a listening ear, giving them useful feedback, and leading them in monitoring their progress over time. Certainly, teachers can be reflective without help from literacy coaches—and teachers usually are—but literacy coaches can facilitate that reflection and make teaching a less lonely profession.

Literacy coaching honors adult learners. Adult learners like to have a say in their learning and to have the learning process respond directly to their needs. In addition, many adults are aware of how they learn best, and most adults want their learning to be directly applicable to their lives. The literacy coaching process honors the way adults learn by responding to teachers' needs and supporting them as they learn about topics and issues that they have selected. In addition, literacy coaching supports teachers' growth in a variety of ways, according to teachers' styles of learning, and literacy coaching allows teachers to apply and test what they are learning in the day-to-day work that they do in their classrooms.

Literacy coaching leads to student achievement. An increasing number of studies are demonstrating that coaching leads to increased student achievement: Joyce and Showers have done the most to address the issue of coaching in general. Their work in the 1980s and 1990s demonstrated that coaching did indeed contribute to student achievement (Joyce & Showers, 1988; Joyce, Murphy, Showers, & Murphy, 1989). In the specific area of literacy, a study by the Foundation for California Early Literacy Learning (Swartz, Shook, & Klein, 2001) demonstrated that coaching had a positive effect on young students' literacy achievement. In addition, Killion (2003) reports that ongoing support for teachers was found to be essential in effective literacy programs, although that support varied from what might be called true literacy coaching to more superficial forms of support. Lyons and Pinnell (1999) report positive effects of coaching on literacy learning, and Norton (2001) provides a study showing that student writing improves dramatically as a result of a professional development model focused on coaching. In addition, Lapp, Fisher, Flood, and Frey (2003) describe a program in three high-poverty San Diego schools that included literacy coaching as 50% of reading specialists' duties and that led to a marked increase in student achievement.

Literacy coaching serves many purposes. It supports significant instructional change and increased teacher reflection, which contributes to the reshaping of school cultures. It supports teacher professional development in a manner that honors the manner in which adults learn best. Above all, literacy coaching contributes to increased student achievement in literacy. Given all of the reasons for literacy coaching, the need for literacy coaches is increasing rapidly.

The Need for Literacy Coaching

Literacy coaching has valuable purposes, and you and I are not the only ones who have discovered this fact. The demand for literacy coaches has grown rapidly in the past few years. I have searched for statistics on the number of literacy coaches, but the statistics do not exist. However, I do have circumstantial evidence that the demand is on the rise. The following are a few of the signs of the growth of literacy coaching.

Reading First. The Reading First portion of the federal No Child Left Behind Act of 2001 states that literacy coaching should be a part of the professional development in all Reading First schools. At the time of this writing, all 50 U.S. states, plus the District of Columbia, American Samoa, and the Bureau of Indian Affairs, have applied for Reading First grants, and many schools are already implementing them.

Head Start. The U.S. Department of Health and Human Services has mandated that all Head Start programs include literacy coaching in their professional development.

Major initiatives. Organizations that provide leadership in education have demonstrated a commitment to literacy coaching. For instance, in its effort to improve the achievement of adolescent learners, the Alliance for Excellent Education has funded a major paper on literacy coaching (Sturtevant, 2003). In California, the Bay Area School Reform Collaborative (BASRC) has made a significant commitment to literacy coaching as a key component of school change in the 28 school districts it serves, with additional support from organizations such as the William and Flora Hewlett Foundation, the Annenberg Foundation, and the Consortium of Reading Excellence (CORE).

School districts. School districts throughout the United States and beyond have adopted literacy coaching as a key component of professional development. The list of such school districts includes large urban districts, such as Denver and Boston, and small districts such as those in Walker County, Georgia, and Ship Rock, New Mexico.

Secondary-level literacy coaches. Although literacy coaching at the secondary level is just starting to gain attention, the need for such coaches has already been recognized. The Alliance for Excellent Education's recently published white paper (Sturtevant, 2003) indicates that as many as 10,000 literacy coaches are needed in order to meet the literacy achievement needs of adolescent learners.

Thus, the need for literacy coaching is evident across the United States, at all levels of schooling, and in many educational settings. Coaching is seen as an important method for improving literacy instruction and literacy achievement. However, the value and need for coaching is best understood in the context of school reform.

The Context of Literacy Coaching

The value of literacy coaching and the demand for literacy coaching have been created in a social context that suggests that schools are broken and that a significant part of the problem lies with teachers (see, for instance, the Teacher Quality components of the Comprehensive School Reform legislation and of the No Child Left Behind Act of 2001). When describing public schools, the media and the public frequently perceive bad teaching that leads to crisis-ridden schools. Literacy coaches are a means for overcoming this crisis by improving teaching. This view is influenced by the political and theoretical lenses through which public education is viewed. There are other such lenses that could be used, and they would provide a different view of the so-called education crisis. For instance, one might look at today's educational milieu and instead see hard-working teachers beating the odds for student populations beset by inequity, oppression, and poverty. Or one might perceive schools as dysfunctional systems in which the mere survival of the children and the adults who work in them is a remarkable feat. Or one might observe instructional programs and materials that are poorly aligned with assessments and, therefore, are not adequately recognized for teaching what they do. There are more possible views, but these examples are no doubt adequate for demonstrating the complexity of education and the unrecognized choices that are made when one accepts a coaching model of teacher professional development.

The irony of literacy coaching is that, even though it grows out of the "fix-the-teacher-and-fix-the-schools" perspective, it is valuable in supporting teachers and in helping teachers to do the good things that they have always done. In addition, literacy coaches can help teachers identify problems and work to solve them—something good teachers do without coaching help but which can be done even more successfully with support. And literacy coaches can assist schools in being the kinds of places that prove conventional wisdom wrong—in other words, that prove that schools are not hopelessly broken.

I encourage literacy coaches to avoid naiveté. Literacy coaches should recognize that literacy coaching is seen as valuable for different purposes depending on the perspective of the beholder. In addition, it is essential for literacy coaches to recognize that the work of improving education does not lie entirely with them and that the complexities of schools and society mean that when students struggle there are myriad forces at work, and teachers should not be blamed. To avoid such blame, and to maximize literacy coaching in the complex context of school reform, literacy coaches need to be insightful, communicative, and skilled. This book will help develop these characteristics.

The Organization of This Book

To make this book accessible, I've divided it into sections consisting of a few chapters each. I've also provided a list of questions at the beginning of each chapter to indicate which of your questions that chapter will answer. These questions also are listed by topic in an appendix.

The rest of the book consists primarily of three sections. Each section addresses a major group of questions that literacy coaches usually pose. The questions corresponding to the first section of this book address change. What is it, and how does it happen? Change is the reason for literacy coaching: If educators wanted the status quo, they wouldn't seek literacy coaches.

Therefore, we need to consider some issues about change. In chapter 1, I provide a summary of researchers' recommendations for improving school change. In addition, I help you think about the aspects of education upon which you might focus your literacy coaching efforts. This information is important to consider and to share with others, especially with school principals, because literacy coaching looks very different if you are trying to change, say, cognition, than if you are trying to change, say, the school culture.

Chapter 2 presents my understanding of change in a way that I hope will provoke you to consider change differently. I am concerned that most educators think of change as episodic, universally applicable, and traumatic, and I don't believe it has to be so.

Another set of questions, corresponding with the second section of the book, addresses the duties and roles of literacy coaches. In this section, we get down to the practical matters of starting out, selecting formats for coaching, and approaching problems in the most helpful manner. Chapters 3 and 4 will help you create the foundation for your literacy coaching work by ensuring that you start out on the right foot and maximize the talents you bring to the job. Chapter 5 will add useful communication practices to your repertoire of literacy coaching skills. Finally, chapters 6 and 7 will give you the tools you need to do the essential tasks of your job.

A third set of questions, often the most difficult and most frequent, addresses the challenges and obstacles faced by literacy coaches. These questions are addressed in section 3. Chapter 8 will help you approach difficult situations with teachers. Chapter 9 will assist you with additional problems and questions that may arise, and chapter 10 will give you a comfortable set of resources to fall back on when faced with difficult situations.

I end the book with three important pieces. First, the conclusion offers an overview of activities to do and to avoid as a literacy coach. Then, Appendix A lists by topic the questions addressed by each chapter of the book. Finally, the narrative bibliography in Appendix B provides a discussion of references to which you can refer for more information on the many topics I address throughout the book.

I'd like to add a bit more about resources and references. As an author, I strive always to give credit to others whose ideas I use in my work. I do that in this book, using typical reference citations, when I specifically refer to others' work. However, much of what I write about in this book is not taken directly from the work of others, but rather reflects my own work in the field and in theorizing and researching literacy coaching. On the other hand, my thinking is influenced by a wide range of reading that I have done. I would like to make you aware of that reading, both to acknowledge the contribution of other authors and to help you understand how my ideas have evolved. My concern is that, if I fill the main part of the book with references to a lot of additional sources, the book may become less user friendly. I've resolved this dilemma in two ways. First, I've included a few key resources at the end of each chapter, which will provide you with additional ideas or background information. In addition, I've provided information about additional sources in the narrative bibliography. I've attempted in this narrative bibliography to continue to "talk" to you, the reader, rather than just list resources. I hope that style is helpful and engaging. And, of course, I provide a traditional list of references at the end of the book.

Conclusion

There is no doubt in my mind that literacy coaching is an effective model and that the need for literacy coaches is great. A book such as this will assist literacy coaches in doing the job that lies before them.

ADDITIONAL RESOURCES FOR LITERACY COACHES

Black, C. (2002). *Get over it! Education reform is dead. Now what?* Portsmouth, NH: Heinemann.

Corrie, L. (1995). The structure and culture of staff collaboration: Managing meaning and opening doors. *Educational Review, 47*(1), 89–99.

Flaherty, J. (1999). *Coaching: Evoking excellence in others.* Boston: Butterworth-Heinemann.

Rodgers, E.M., &. Pinnell, G.S. (Eds.). (2002). *Learning from teaching in literacy education: New perspectives on professional development.* Portsmouth, NH: Heinemann.

Showers, B., & Joyce, B. (1996). The evolution of peer coaching. *Educational Leadership, 53*(6), 12–16.

Sweeney, D. (2003). *Learning along the way: Professional development by and for teachers.* Portland, ME: Stenhouse.

How Do I Promote Change?

CHAPTER 1

What Do the Experts Say About Educational Change?

- Does change begin with the teacher, the principal, what is being changed, or how the change is being implemented? Which is most important?

- What have researchers suggested as the focus of change?

- How can I understand the differing perspectives of my principal, the teachers, and myself?

Literacy coaches are in the change business. Their jobs wouldn't exist if someone didn't want someone else to change. We speak frequently about change in education, and often that speech becomes reduced to maxims. For instance, many of us have heard a speaker, administrator, or facilitator say that "Change takes time," "Change is a process," and "It is painful to change." However, for all the easy phrases and loud pronouncements about change, and all of the presumed agreement that something needs to change, educators don't often consider the details of change.

This chapter provides an overview of the approaches to educational change that have taken place in the last 40 years. It also delineates the areas in which change is typically focused. This overview is important to literacy coaches for the following reasons:

- Understanding current conceptions of change enables literacy coaches to understand what the educators they work with may be thinking and expecting.

- Having an overview of the myriad approaches to change enables literacy coaches to avoid falling into the trap that any one approach will provide *the* solution.

- Knowing about the areas upon which change can focus will broaden the perspectives of literacy coaches, school administrators, and teachers as they plan for literacy changes.

• Becoming familiar with approaches to educational change that address various focus areas will give literacy coaches the ability to adapt their methods to the nature of the staff's goals.

My work with literacy coaches has led me to understand that as long as they hold inaccurate and sometimes harmful notions about change, they will be ineffective and frustrated. When I work with literacy coaches, I know they are eager to talk about practical matters, and sometimes they are frustrated when I suggest we talk about change first. But this thinking and rethinking about change helps them tremendously in considering how to best perform the practical aspects of their jobs. I hope it will help you, too.

Technologies of Change

Over the years, experts in educational change have focused their attentions on four elements of change: (1) who will lead the change, typically principals; (2) who will implement the change, typically teachers; (3) what will be changed, that is, the innovation; and (4) how the change will occur, that is, the process. Although some of these experts have looked at all four elements in varying degrees, many experts have isolated one of the elements and given their attention to it alone, or have looked at all the elements but in isolation from the other elements. The implication is that there is one most important element that, when attended to, will make the change process smooth and effective or that the various elements can be addressed separately rather than as aspects of a system.

Those of us who have worked in schools for many years tend to understand that change is indeed complex and that we can't focus on just one element of it. That's what some leading educational theorists have concluded, too. Two of them, Huberman and Miles (1986), have said that there is a "cottage industry" of change (p. 61). I agree: Many individuals are trying to "fix" schools by finding *the* solution. However, it just isn't that simple.

Nonetheless, I'd like to review some of the ideas presented by those who address these four elements of change. Taken together, they represent the range of suggestions for how to accomplish change, which provides a good overview. In addition, the length of this list demonstrates the number of ideas educators have been exposed to regarding change. These ideas are familiar to most teachers and administrators and, therefore, what follows is a good reminder that as educators we have been told many times how to change, each time with a different angle. Many of the following educational change ideas are compatible, but some aren't. Also, the number and variety of these ideas may seem overwhelming, so it's no wonder that many educators are confused and frustrated. (See Appendix B for a list of sources in which you can read more about each of the proposed technologies of change.)

Change leadership. Many theories and practical suggestions have been developed regarding how school leaders can manage change more successfully. The focus of most of these suggestions is that the principal must set a tone and direction. Such efforts may take the form of developing a vision; shaping the school culture; fostering a learning community among students; modeling moral, value-oriented behaviors; or developing strategies for the school to follow. In each of these cases, the attention is on the manner in which the principal shapes the others or environments, not on shaping him- or herself. In all cases, the principal influences change not so much by his or her own changed behavior as an end to itself as by his or her own changed behavior leading to changed behavior in others.

Change implementers. The role of teachers in the change process has also been thoroughly dissected. The suggestions in this regard focus on teachers' attitudes and beliefs and on their behaviors. In the category of attitudes and beliefs, the recommendations include that (a) teachers should view themselves as learners in a community of learners; (b) teachers should perceive the connections between their experiences and cultures and their beliefs and practices; and (c) teachers should focus on their philosophies before their activities. In the category of behaviors, the suggestions include that (a) teachers must interact and communicate and (b) teachers must plan and act to meet goals established by their school districts.

The innovation itself. An innovation is the new idea or practice that is being implemented. A variety of kinds of innovations have been presented as *the* answer by various individuals and organizations, including curriculum innovations in disciplinary areas, such as hands-on math or literature-based reading; curriculum innovations focused on learning processes, such as dimensions of learning (Marzano, 1992) or multiple intelligences (Gardner, 1983); innovations in evaluation, such as portfolio assessment; innovations that rethink the role of learners, such as those that consider learners to be knowledge workers (Schlechty, 1990) or constructers of meaning; and innovations that implement ideologies, such as values education or liberatory pedagogy.

The process. The process of educational change also has been analyzed at length. In fact, it would appear that this is the area of change in which the most has been written. Among the suggestions for manipulating this variable are to change behaviors by using a mastery learning model, which emphasizes discrete steps in teaching, testing what was taught, and reteaching; focus on teachers' thinking rather than practices; respond to teachers' attitudes and concerns about the innovation; use a model of teacher inquiry; address school systems; and adapt the school culture.

These six suggestions about changing processes rely upon approaches that vary depending upon the kind of change that is desired. The rest of this chapter reviews considerations about *what* is being changed (e.g., behaviors, thoughts, attitudes, teacher learning processes, systems, or cultures) and how literacy coaches might address the *what* by adjusting the *how* of change.

What Are You Trying to Change?

Let's go back to the example of exercising, which I used in the Introduction. When a person starts an exercise program, it helps if he or she has a clear reason for exercising. Is it to gain flexibility so he or she is less likely to fall? Is it to lose 10 pounds? Is it to lose 50 pounds? Is it to have stronger legs for roller blading? Depending upon what he or she is trying to change, the exerciser will follow a different regimen.

Similarly, literacy coaches may be trying to change a variety of conditions. Some literacy coaches want teachers to implement a single program or initiative adopted by the school district. Some literacy coaches are assigned to coach new teachers or teachers who have been put on plans of assistance. Some literacy coaches are trying to help individual teachers increase student achievement. Some literacy coaches are trying to change the way an entire school staff does its work. And many literacy coaches are expected to do all of the previously mentioned tasks. Clearly, literacy coaches will engage in varied coaching activities depending on the focus of the desired changes.

This matter is made even more complex by the fact that principals, school district administrators, teachers, and others may have their own ideas about what literacy coaches should change. When these people are looking for different changes than the literacy coach is, problems can ensue. For instance, a literacy coach may be trying to change teachers' thinking by assisting them in making decisions based on students' in-process reading behaviors. Meanwhile, a principal may want the literacy coach to help the entire staff implement a new basal series. These competing change goals can cause problems.

The purpose of this section, then, is to review the areas upon which literacy coaches might focus their change efforts. This will clarify what's possible and what may be expected from literacy coaches and will also assist literacy coaches in starting to think about the approaches they will use in their coaching work.

Several perspectives about what should be changed can be found in the educational literature. Some of these perspectives are compatible and others are contradictory. Literacy coaches will find it helpful to be familiar with all of them. In this way, coaches will have a number of lenses through which they can understand the focus of change and through which they can consider the situations in which they work. You might think about change at your school in one way that serves you well much of the time, but in some situations in which your usual frame of reference does not seem productive, it will help to have some additional perspectives to refer to.

In addition, literacy coaches will benefit from understanding a number of approaches to change because their colleagues may hold a variety of perspectives. It will be helpful to literacy coaches if they can spot a different focus for change among colleagues. For example, if a principal believes that change is a matter of changing behaviors, and you as literacy coach believe it's a matter of changing thinking, recognizing this difference will help the two of you discuss your views and work more productively together.

The following sections briefly discuss the six perspectives on change: (1) change focused on behavior, (2) change focused on attitude, (3) change focused on cognition, (4) change focused on inquiry, (5) change focused on systems, and (6) change focused on culture.

Change Focused on Behavior

Some change efforts emphasize the behavior of participants. These efforts make explicit the behaviors that are desired and the method that will be used to gauge such behaviors. Traditional supervision models often have used behavior-focused approaches. For example, a principal might state that he or she wants to see writing taught in every classroom. The gauge of change is whether the appropriate behavior—in this case, teaching writing—can be observed when the principal visits the classrooms.

When a change in behavior is the goal, literacy coaches will want to make clear the following points:

- the desired behavior(s) (e.g., all teachers will use running records)
- how the desired behavior(s) will look and/or sound in a classroom, or the frequency of the behavior (e.g., a running record will be recorded during an individual conference for each child at least monthly)
- how the behavior will improve student achievement (e.g., the running record will guide teachers in providing instruction targeted at students' instructional needs)

Many behavior-focused approaches will include rewards for those who demonstrate the desired behaviors and/or punishments for those who don't. Because literacy coaches are not supervisors, they may not wish to get involved with reward or punishment systems.

Change Focused on Attitude

The best example of a change perspective that focuses on attitude is the Concerns-Based Adoption Model (CBAM) (Hord, 1987). This perspective suggests that it is participants' attitudes toward a proposed innovation that matters when one attempts to promote change. The levels of concern in the CBAM are enumerated. Each of the following levels is described by an individual's stance toward a proposed innovation:

- Level 0: The teacher knows nothing about the innovation.
- Level 1: The teacher is collecting information to learn about the innovation.
- Level 2: The teacher is wondering how the innovation will affect her personally—will she have enough time, will it sap her energy, and other questions.
- Level 3: The teacher is trying to address practical issues raised by the innovation—fitting it in the schedule, managing the materials, and others.
- Level 4: The teacher is determining the effect—positive, negative, or nonexistent—the innovation is having on her goals, particularly student achievement.
- Level 5: The teacher is interested in elaborating upon the innovation, making modifications and fitting it into other goals or programs, and sometimes sharing ideas with others.
- Level 6: The teacher is satisfied with the innovation and interested in moving on to new problems and questions, perhaps those that are raised by the innovation itself.

A coach familiar with the CBAM might notice the attitudes of teachers when presented, say, with guided reading as a new component of the literacy program. Is a teacher saying that she is not interested (Level 1), asking questions about where to fit it into her already-crowded day (Level 3), or excited about sharing how she is already implementing guided reading (Level 5)? The literacy coach would respond differently to each level of concern. For instance, if a teacher had no interest in guided reading, the literacy coach might listen for an opportunity to suggest guided reading as an option and to explain why it might be useful. On the other hand, if a teacher is concerned about fitting guided reading into her already crowded day, the literacy coach might ask the teacher if they could look at the teacher's daily schedule in order to work together to find a place for guided reading.

Change Focused on Cognition

The emphasis in some change endeavors is participants' cognition. These efforts attempt to get participants to change their thinking by building a trusting relationship in which the literacy coach or other participants are viewed as valued colleagues. From this standpoint, participants feel comfortable challenging their own ideas and learning from one other.

The notion of cognitive dissonance (Festinger, 1957) is important to this perspective. This term refers to an individual's discomfort when faced with two seemingly incompatible ideas. For instance, a teacher may have the understanding that round-robin reading is a productive use of class time and may also have the understanding that students cannot understand what was read during round-robin reading. This creates cognitive dissonance. In a trusting environment, that teacher will be able to learn new information to resolve this cognitive conflict. A literacy coach can play a significant role in this new learning by asking important questions, providing information, and giving the teacher feedback on the teaching process used.

Viewing change as a process of changing one's understanding is perhaps the most common view among literacy coaches. Many literacy coaches believe that their role is one of changing teachers' thinking. Although this is an important role, it is usually not adequate. Teaching is not merely a reflection of one's thinking. Rather, teaching is influenced by one's beliefs, values, perceptions, and experiences, as well as by the context of the particular teaching act. Therefore, literacy coaches are encouraged to learn not only about coaching the thinking of others but also to combine such efforts with other perspectives on change.

Change Focused on Inquiry

When educators view change as inquiry, they emphasize the *process* used to find new understandings and practices. According to Hubbard and Power (1993), this process includes the following characteristics:

- It is driven by questions asked by the participants (usually teachers but sometimes parents, administrators, students, or community members).

- It begins with extensive data collection. Such data might include student work samples; surveys of students, teachers, parents, or others; test scores; peer and self-observations; or any other evidence that sheds light on the inquiry.
- It includes the reading of professional literature related to the topic.
- It may include consulting with others in the field (colleagues at other schools or in other districts, university researchers, regional educational laboratories, or experts in content areas such as science or social studies disciplines).
- An extensive review of data and information collected, combined with extensive reflection and discussion among participants, leads to hypotheses.
- Hypotheses are used to develop new practices, about which additional data are collected.
- The process continues until the inquiry leads to desired changes.

Literacy coaching of this kind takes time and commitment. However, those who participate in an inquiry process usually find it highly rewarding, because inquiry is a catalyst for teacher reflection and because inquiry guides teachers to make instructional decisions based on a range of data. In addition, the process of inquiry affects the school culture by promoting collaborative problem solving.

Change Focused on Systems

Educational leaders who think about change have learned from physicists and others who study systems. *System* refers to a network of units—be they cells, neighborhoods, family members, or members of a teaching staff—that together has one purpose: to continue to exist. When a system is healthy, each component (for example, each teacher) contributes to the well-being of the system; all contribute for the mutual benefit of all. When a system is unhealthy, it contorts to maintain its existence, and each member contributes to the contortion.

For example, when a new textbook series is adopted by a school district, the staffs at two high schools in that school district might approach the adoption differently based on the system inherent to those staffs. In one school, where the staff has succeeded in cooperating and in helping students to succeed, this disruption in their system—that is, the introduction of the new textbook—may create some struggles, but the system maintains its health. In order to maintain the system's health, one staff member might volunteer to become a building leader, organizing the new books and related materials and scheduling meetings to discuss how the implementation is going. Another staff member, who is good at quickly finding what is wrong, may begin sharing her solutions to some trouble spots and work with a colleague to develop a new record-keeping procedure. And on it goes, until the system of cooperation and success has restored itself.

In the other school, where the staff has succeeded in mistrusting one another and in blaming the students for their lack of success, the adoption also disrupts the system for a brief time. Soon, though, a building leader who complains loudly to parents about what he or she doesn't like has created alarm at a school board meeting, and a teacher who is good at quickly finding what is wrong begins telling others that the school district administration is trying to destroy the strong educational program that they previously had. Very quickly, the system of mistrust and blame is returned.

A literacy coach's role, from a systems perspective, includes providing assistance to a school staff in examining broad issues, such as how the staff functions and how it would like to work. These are difficult activities and best done when the principal is involved. Another use of a systems perspective for a literacy coach is the understanding that any change in a system produces other changes in the system, with equilibrium—that is, returning to "normal"—as the ultimate goal. If a staff is unhealthy, this means that the literacy coach needs to be realistic about the effect he or she can have.

Change Focused on Culture

Both systems-focused change and culture-focused change approaches recognize that organizations often need to be different at the macro (e.g., school) level before they can be different at the micro (e.g., teaching-strategy) level. When culture is the focus of change, the emphasis is often upon relationships and processes. Building trust is essential (although it is important for each of the previously discussed perspectives on change as well), and staff processes that engage and empower often are the tools for bringing about cultural change in a trusting environment.

Literacy coaches can't change school cultures by themselves. The entire school staff must be committed to such efforts, and the principal must provide strong leadership. However, a literacy coach who is familiar with culture-focused change can ask important questions, such as the following:

- How do we want to solve problems when they arise in our new literacy program?
- How will we decide how to share limited resources?
- What kind of readers and writers do we want to come out of our school?

- What information should we share with one another about what we do in our own classrooms?

Questions of this kind are powerful in their ability to raise awareness of "how things are done around here." And when usual procedures are made visible, the potential exists for culture to change.

The six areas upon which change are focused provide six different challenges for literacy coaches. When one considers that the focus of change could be teachers' behavior, teachers' attitudes, teachers' thinking, teachers' learning, systems in the school, or the school culture, one can understand the importance of determining *what* is being changed. Literacy coaches cannot make this decision on their own. They need to work with principals, teachers, and other school staff members to determine the desired focus of change.

Conclusion

Research on educational change often focuses on four areas of change: the change leader, the change implementer, the change itself, and the process of change. At times this research makes it seem as though there is a "technology of change" that spells out exactly what variable to manipulate in order to achieve the desired end. Of course, such an approach oversimplifies change as well as the thinking of the researchers, but it is just such approaches that lead educators to attempt a one-size-fits-all or a this-is-*the*-answer approach. Literacy coaches benefit from knowing about the components that researchers have identified as contributing to educational change.

Practitioners, in the meantime, have developed a range of approaches to change based on what is being changed. For instance, if teacher thinking is the focus of change, then a cognitive coaching approach may work best, whereas if the decision-making process is being changed, then a process focused on systems may work best. Literacy coaches are wise to clarify the focus (or foci) of change and to develop approaches to change that mesh with it.

After reading this chapter, literacy coaches may want to ask the following questions:

- What does my principal think is the focus of change in our school? What do the teachers think? What do I think?
- How can I ensure that all of us on this staff share the same focus for change? If I can't, how can I address competing foci?
- Are there processes for change that will fit better with the focus of change?

ADDITIONAL RESOURCES FOR LITERACY COACHES

Blanchard, K., Lacinak, T., Tompkins, C., & Ballard, J. (2002). *Whale done! The power of positive relationships.* New York: Free Press.

Cochran-Smith, M., & Lytle, S.L. (Eds.). (1993). *Inside/Outside: Teacher research and knowledge.* New York: Teachers College Press.

Costa, A.L., & Garmston, R.J. (2002). *Cognitive coaching: A foundation for Renaissance schools* (2nd ed.). Norwood, MA: Christopher-Gordon.

Hord, S.M., Rutherford, W.L., Huling-Austin, L., & Hall, G. (1987). *Taking charge of change.* Alexandria, VA: Association for Supervision and Curriculum Development.

Sarason, S.B. (1996). *Revisiting "The culture of the school and the problem of change."* New York: Teachers College Press.

Wheatley, M.J., & Kellner-Rogers, M. (1999). *A simpler way.* San Francisco: Barrett-Koehler.

CHAPTER 2

Why Is Change So Difficult?

- How can I understand teachers who seem to resist change?

- How does a literacy coach act as a change agent?

- Why is it so painful for a staff to change?

- Why can't we look at a school that has changed successfully and then just copy what it did?

Conventional wisdom in education is as follows: Change is difficult and painful. Some teachers want to change and readily do so, but many resist and make life miserable for all of those who want to move ahead. It is important to plan for change and then implement the plan in a step-by-step manner until the change is completed. Change depends on one or more change agents who create the vision and support educators in doing what wouldn't get done otherwise.

These statements may be accurate in some instances, but in many instances they aren't. What's more, the assumptions behind such statements—for instance, that there are "good" and "bad" teachers, change is something many resist, change has a discrete beginning and end, and a change agent "creates" change—are frequently harmful and lead to stereotypes. Often the literacy coaches with whom I work make mistakes because they are operating under these assumptions (and a few others to be addressed in later chapters). By buying into conventional wisdom about change, literacy coaches approach their work with unnecessary negativity and fear, and they—and the teachers with whom they work—make assumptions about the literacy coaches' roles and the beliefs about teachers upon which the literacy coaches are basing their work.

This chapter dispels some of the myths about change. It is possible that some readers will pass by this chapter, believing it is just background information. I'd encourage all readers to read this chapter and come back to it periodically because I believe rethinking change is one of the underpinnings of a literacy coach's success.

Changing Our Understanding of Change

Change Is Constant

The suggestions for creating educational change outlined in chapter 1—the technologies of change—imply that change is *an event*, something with a beginning and an end, something that others control and manipulate, and something in which individuals choose or decline participation. It's as if change is the baseball of education. I can imagine a humorous scenario in which an announcer's voice spreads over a stadium, something like this:

> OK, folks, it's a big night here at Jefferson Elementary Field. First up to the plate, it's Balanced Literacy. Balanced Literacy has been playing well lately, but the other team has recently put Phonics First at the pitcher's mound. It's going to be some game. . . .

To me, however, change isn't an event. It's not even a process. It's a part of existence. To explain, I need to tell a story.

I went back to graduate school after trying to bring about change in several settings and in several roles. While working on my doctorate, I read everything I could get my hands on that had to do with change. (That's how I started the list of technologies of change in chapter 1.) I was looking in particular for an understanding of why some teachers change and some don't. I figured that if we could just understand that, we'd have the magic pill for educational change.

Meanwhile, I was trying to survive as a graduate student, so I occasionally took care of other parts of my life, including my spiritual self. I liked to read books on a range of spiritual perspectives, and one evening I was reading *It's Easier Than You Think: The Buddhist Way to Happiness* (Boorstein, 1995). This book is about Boorstein's understanding of how to live life from a Buddhist perspective.

At one point, I found myself nodding in agreement as I read Boorstein's statement that we are all constantly changing, that life flows like a river and we with it. Suddenly, it occurred to me that this contradicted the work I was doing in my studies. In my professional life, I was looking for forces that start and stop change, but in my personal life, I was viewing change as the constant flow of life. This was a significant moment in my understanding of change.

After all, when you think of it, can you name one moment in your life when change has not taken place? Of course not. Every second, you are growing older, your cells are replacing themselves, your senses are taking in new information, the air and people and world around you revolve and alter. No moment is ever like the one before nor the one after. Yet in schools we conceptualize change as an event, a one-time thing. For instance, we think that teachers learn how to engage students in shared reading and then can move on to the next problem. Not only does this interfere with our approach to change itself, but it also adds to our frustration because it leaves us with the sense that change, if done right, will take place once and then be finished. Then we feel like failures if one change takes place and it leads to the need for another and another and another.

What is different if we think about change as constant? First, we no longer look for starts and stops to change. Change does not become an event; it becomes a "normal" part of the everyday culture of the school. Think about it: When we are advocating for a particular change, we often act as though *that* change is the only change we'll ever need. If someone stopped and asked us, we'd say that that isn't the case, of course, but unless we really do stop and think about it, we often proceed as though the change is the end-all and be-all. For instance, when a literacy coach is trying to convince teachers to implement writing workshop, that implementation may become the focus of the literacy coach's goals. The literacy coach may lose sight of the fact that implementing writing workshop, wonderful as the idea may be, is one change in an ongoing stream of changes. Without this perspective, the literacy coach risks becoming a missionary, rather than a coach. On the other hand, if the coach recognizes that changes in writing instruction are going to be constant and thinks of him- or herself as one who influences those changes by advocating for writing workshop, he or she will try hard but not obsessively to meet this goal.

The perspective that change is constant also leads one to recognize that change is part of everyone's life, even the lives of those teachers who appear resistant to change. At this point, you may be thinking about the teacher who seems stuck and never appears to change. I thought of that kind of teacher, too, when I started to think about change as ongoing for all of us. In particular, I thought about Bob (a pseudonym). Bob was a teacher with whom I worked for several years, and to me he looked pretty stuck. For instance, every year he did the same group activity for his social studies unit on Egypt. His sixth-grade students made a pyramid from cardboard boxes, and it took them weeks to get the project done. Every year, I pondered what instructional purpose the cardboard pyramid served, and every year I concluded that it had very little instructional value. Yet Bob did the same thing, over and over. I once thought to myself that I wouldn't need a calendar if I knew which unit Bob was doing in his classroom; he followed the exact routine and schedule every year, it seemed to me.

One day, Bob came to see me, to ask if I knew anything about when the school district might act on rumored plans to move sixth-grade classes from the elementary schools to the middle schools. "You see," Bob explained, "I'm concerned that if it doesn't happen soon, I might not have the energy to do it. Right now, I change easily, but in a few years I'll be close to retirement, and that might be tough on me." I was stunned. Bob thought that he changed easily!

A few years later, when I was thinking about these matters in graduate school, I thought about Bob with a wider perspective, and here's what occurred to me: At the time of our conversation about middle school, Bob had just seen his only daughter off to college. In addition, he had just dealt with the death of a relative who was living in his home. Bob had a great deal of change going on in his life; it just wasn't easily visible at work.

I have concluded that individuals change at their own rates, and those who don't seem to be changing are probably just doing it in a way that is not easily perceived. The changes may be internal or be taking place in a different setting, or perhaps these individuals change at a pace that makes it hard to see the changes unless they are observed over a long period of time.

If change is always happening, though, then school leaders, including literacy coaches, don't have to try to be change agents in the sense that they *create* change. Change is already happening and will continue without assistance. Rather, we may serve to direct, focus, speed up, or even slow down changes that are occurring. Think of sunshine coming through a magnifying glass. We can't control the sun, but we can focus its rays. In a similar manner, literacy coaches can provide resources, demonstrations, workshops, and conversations that lead and support the changes taking place.

One final insight that results from this new view of change is that, given that change is ongoing and everywhere, it is not totally in our control, and we'll only frustrate ourselves and others if we try to make it so. Again, I think of a metaphor, this time a rosebush. If I decide to plant a rosebush in my yard, I may have an image of what I want it to look like. That image will probably include perfectly shaped and colored roses, evenly spaced and regularly blooming on a shrub that is a certain height and perfectly fills a space in my yard. However, I will probably never achieve that exact rose bush, and if I do, it won't last. The forces of rain, wind, sunshine, drought, my forgetfulness, neighborhood children and dogs, and so on will prevent the bush from being perfect. It doesn't hurt me to have an idea in my mind of the rosebush I want: The vision will encourage me to tend to the rosebush and do my best to change it into that vision. But I'll be frustrated and perhaps even harm the bush if I become overly committed to making that perfect vision a reality.

The same idea is true for literacy instruction and programs. As a literacy coach, you might have a vision of what a good program looks and sounds like. In fact, I hope you do and encourage you to develop one if you don't. However, given the constant forces that will influence your attempts to get there, and the forces that will continue to act even if you do get there, you're doomed to frustration and failure if you hold too tightly to that vision. Change is ongoing in schools, and you can't rein it in to make it yours. Even if you accomplish what you aimed for, the constancy of change means that it, too, will pass.

Change Is Situated

A question was posed recently on a listserv for teacher educators. The author asked, What would it take to "fix" public education? My response to this question is that first, we need to stop asking it. The question implies that there is one way to make schools better, and I believe this one-size-fits-all mentality is part of the problem. Those of you who have been educators for a while have seen it happen over and over again: Every few years we learn of the next new thing that purportedly will save us all. However, within a few years (or occasionally, a few months), the new thing dies out and is replaced with something else, leaving in its wake the sense that the old innovation was mistakenly labeled a good idea and now we need to move on to the one that really *is*.

If you've been in education a while, you also know that many of the innovations that came and went had merit. I'd suggest that the reason they didn't last is because we think of change as something that is universally the same. In other words, if an innovation is valuable, it has to work everywhere. Actually, researcher Larry Cuban (1988) has found that teachers don't think this way. Teachers generally believe an innovation has value if it is flexible enough to be adapted to a variety of settings. Cuban found, though, that others—policymakers and the public, for instance—think the opposite. To them, an innovation is valuable if it can be implemented consistently across settings and yield consistent results across those settings (1998). And, of course, educators are vastly outnumbered by the general public.

Teachers are practical people, and teachers base a lot of their learning on action research, even though they don't always label it as such. They see a problem in their classroom, they make some changes, and they see if those changes have been effective. This is the crux of action research. And among the things that teachers learn from their action research is that many innovations work with some classes and not with others, or work with some children and not others, or work for some teachers and not others.

A good example of such an innovation would be literacy centers. I work with some teachers who love having literacy centers in their classrooms and couldn't imagine a reading workshop without them. Other teachers find literacy centers to be overwhelming for them and their students and prefer to have students read and journal during the part of reading workshop when the teachers might otherwise engage children in literacy centers. And some of these teachers change their opinions from year to year based on their classrooms, the level of additional support they have (resource teachers, student teachers, etc.), and their own energy levels.

However, those who write about reading workshop may make claims that it always includes literacy centers, or it always includes silent reading and journaling. Teachers who want to change their literacy instruction may believe that they *must* include one or the other; therefore, some teachers will be successful and others won't.

If educators think about change as situated—meaning that it depends on myriad shifting factors—the number of teachers succeeding at their attempted changes will increase. What's more, if educators remember that changes need adjustments in each situation and over time, the changes that are made are more likely to continue to lead to success.

Change Occurs When One Is Safe or Traumatized

It seems as though there is no middle ground for change. It occurs in safe environments and in unsafe ones. For example, I love to bicycle, and a couple of years ago, I decided to train for a six-day, 540-mile bike ride from St. Paul, Minnesota, to Chicago, Illinois, to raise money for AIDS charities. I had never done anything like this, and I spent months in training. One of the best sources of support that I had was an electronic mailing list of other riders, some of whom were new to that kind of riding, just like me, and some of whom had previously done rides like the one for which I was preparing. One of my concerns was how I would manage on the hilly portions of the route because the area of central Illinois in which I live is flat. I posted a question to the electronic mailing list and got great advice from someone who called himself Carbon Lord—the highest quality and fastest bicycles are made of carbon. He gave me detailed advice on how to manage hills, advice which enabled me to make it up all the hills on the ride. There were 1700 bicyclists on that six-day ride, so I never caught up with Carbon Lord, but I learned at the end of the week that he had finished first on every single day of the ride. Clearly, this guy was a master, yet his friendly and encouraging suggestions had still enabled me to learn from him and change significantly as a rider.

Another force that also changed me as a rider was a resident of a county road outside my town. This resident was a big dog. On one of my first training rides, this dog appeared suddenly beside me and, probably responding to some border collie genes in him, attempted to "herd" me with his body. I was knocked off my bike and had injuries serious enough to send me to the emergency room. I changed a lot as a rider because of this traumatic event. I never ride in the country without spray to ward off aggressive dogs; I have learned to make my voice strong in yelling "No," or "Stay" to dogs running after me; and I have learned to watch for dogs as I approach every farm along the way.

My bicycle training exemplifies the two ways most of us experience change: (1) as part of a supportive relationship or (2) as the result of trauma. Have you ever changed significantly in any other way?

I believe this is why supervisors have a hard time getting people to change. In education, most supervisors don't want to traumatize teachers, so they use gentler methods of overseeing the teachers. These traditional supervisory methods—such as goal setting, observation checklists, lesson plan monitoring, and improvement plan use—are often ineffective. They provoke stress, a condition under which most workers become less effective, and although they may produce superficial changes, they don't produce long-term changes because they are neither sufficiently supportive nor sufficiently traumatic.

For example, principal Beth Jones may develop an improvement plan with teacher Donna Smith in which Donna will post a word wall in her room. Donna may create the word wall but then only draw children's attention to it when Beth is in the room. This isn't much of a change. Acting as a supervisor, Beth's only real means of assuring change may be to traumatize Donna. If Beth's commitment to demanding change is strong enough, she may place Donna on a "plan of assistance," demand that Donna change grades or buildings, or threaten to fire Donna.

At this point you may be thinking, Wait a minute! That's not fair! There are many effective principals who support teacher change! I agree. But I don't believe they do it by acting as supervisors. As supervisors, they'll achieve change only by creating an upheaval, causing individuals, groups, or entire staffs to feel traumatized. Rather, the principals who are most effective in supporting change do just that—they support it.

Supporting change is different from acting like the boss and demanding it. When a teacher is supported in making changes, the environment is safe. He or she can try things, take chances, and make mistakes. A key to a supportive environment is supportive relationships with others. Although nature or pets can indeed make us feel supported, making significant change usually requires supportive relationships with humans.

As for traumatic change, it can be effective. If you've had a car accident while making a left turn at a corner, you probably have changed into a driver who is careful when making left turns. If you had a spouse or partner suddenly leave you, you probably have become more cautious about relationships with significant others. Although these kinds of traumas do induce change, they come with a high price. And who would seek a car accident or divorce for the sake of personal growth? For school leaders, including literacy coaches, the cost of traumatic change can include severed professional relationships, negative reputations that can't be overcome, and an inability to establish trust in the future. The change is rarely worth the cost.

Nonetheless, there are those who think change should be demanded of teachers. Currently, the demands for change are coming in the form of demands for improved test scores. For some educators, these demands are traumatic: Many teachers are burning out, feeling more powerless than ever before in their careers, and looking toward retirement or career changes. For other educators, these demands are not yet traumatic, probably because these teachers work in schools that had stronger test scores to begin with, but that could change over time as the demands increase.

I'd encourage you to think about change as occurring in the context of a safe, supportive environment. It's the only way to achieve true growth—in other words, change that is significant and affirming.

Changing Change

I hope that you consider the ideas I have just presented about change. You don't have to agree with them right away, but think about them for a while and see how you feel. First, you might think about how they describe non-school aspects of change. Do they fit the way you have changed in your relationship to your spouse or partner, in patterns at your place of worship, or in the manner by which you eat and exercise? In other words, do these ideas support or explain efforts to change in other parts of your life?

You might discuss these issues with others at school. The notions are different from what most people have heard for years about change, so bring them up at a time when you and colleagues can really think about them. In other words, don't summarize these ideas as you are collecting your belongings to leave the lunchroom and return to class. Wait for a time when you have a half hour to talk. Now, you may be asking, When do I have a half hour to talk with colleagues? Well, that may be a problem, but it is one worth solving. If you are committed to supporting change in your school, it will be helpful if you discuss with others exactly what they think that means. You also may want to visit with your principal about these matters. If your principal thinks that change is an event and when you have "created" it, your job is finished, and you think change is ongoing, situated, and relational, troubles may arise. While you are busy developing trust, engaging in dialogue, listening and learning, your principal may think you should be telling, monitoring, and correcting. Clearly, these divergent views of change could cause confusion and conflict between you and the principal. By talking about your differing views, you and the principal can understand each other better and perhaps even understand the reasons for each other's views. It is unlikely that a conversation will change the principal's views (or yours, for that matter), but it will begin a dialogue that will help you work together productively. When differences are made visible and acknowledged as acceptable, the parties involved can work together with respect. When differences are ignored, tension and mistrust develop.

In the worst case, if the principal feels strongly about change as an event that you should create, you may have to honor the principal's wishes in order to keep your job. This may make you unhappy and may lead you to seek a different position in the future, but at least you will understand the situation in which you are working. For most literacy coaches, their principal will not be this stubborn, and in most cases the dialogue that is begun will lead to a fruitful increase of understanding and shared perspectives.

Writing an occasional reflection about change might be helpful as well. Again, you might be asking, When does she think I have time to write reflections? Make some time. See it as a job duty, and think of it as an investment in your ability to do the rest of your job well. As you reflect, you might explore questions such as the following:

- What are some changes that I have experienced in my personal life?
- What are some changes that I have experienced in my professional life?
- Can I note beginning and ending points for these changes? If so, what were they?
- What changes have occurred in my life even though I did nothing to make them happen?
- What changes have I intentionally attempted, and how did they go?
- What has facilitated or limited changes I've attempted or accomplished?
- Has there been a time in my personal or professional life when no change was taking place?
- If I think of my job as one of stepping into the ongoing stream of change, rather than starting a change process, how does that change the way I work?

- What would the teachers I work with say about these ideas? How can I make time to ask them and find out?
- Is there someone whom I have labeled as "stuck" or never changing? Is there another way to view them?

Influencing how others see change is a difficult task. I've provided some suggestions here for how a literacy coach might make an attempt at such change. However, I'd encourage you to do so cautiously, and at an easy pace, so you don't become threatening to others in the school. In addition, try not to do this work alone. As my suggestions indicate, a literacy coach needs to bring others into the conversation if change is to be changed in the school.

Conclusion

Rethinking change can help literacy coaches avoid some common mistakes. School leaders often think of change as occurring event by event, in a painful—even traumatic—way, and when they learn about a change that was successful at another school, they trust it will be effective in their school. I would encourage such leaders, including literacy coaches, to think differently.

Change is constant in the lives of everyone, even in those teachers who are not visibly changing in the way school leaders wish them to. Literacy coaches will benefit from remembering that everyone is changing and that one change will only lead to another change. This will help literacy coaches to stop trying to be change agents who instigate a change and see it through to completion. Instead, they will think of themselves as change influencers, like rocks in a running stream that redirect the flow.

Another new way to think of change is that it is situated. When looked at this way, change is no longer a solution that is sought for all schools, all classrooms, all teachers, and all students. Instead, change is sought for the situation at hand, and those involved in the change will be wise to remain open to modifying the change on an as-needed basis.

Finally, change does not have to be traumatic and, in fact, when it is traumatic it brings with it a great risk of damage—to relationships, self-concepts, and the overall success of teachers and schools. On the other hand, when change occurs in a supportive environment that includes trusting relationships, those involved have an easier time committing to it and making the change a lasting part of their work.

The approach a literacy coach takes to change will greatly influence his work. The manner in which the literacy coach conveys his approach to change will greatly influence his success. The following chapter assists literacy coaches in thinking about how they want to approach their work from the beginning.

ADDITIONAL RESOURCES FOR LITERACY COACHES

Hubbard, R.S., & Power, B.M. (1993). *The art of classroom inquiry: A handbook for teacher-researchers*. Portsmouth, NH: Heinemann.

Tyack, D.B., & Cuban, L. (1995). *Tinkering toward utopia: A century of public school reform*. Cambridge, MA: Harvard University Press.

What Does a Successful Literacy Coach Do?

CHAPTER 3

How Do I Begin My Work as a Literacy Coach?

- How can I make a good first impression?
- How do I approach the many kinds of teachers in the school?
- What's the best way to introduce myself to the principal, the staff, and the parents?
- What if my offers of help are met with silence?

"First impressions count": We've all heard this adage, and many of us believe it to one extent or another. In education, first impressions do seem to matter. Think of the chatter among the teachers after the new principal conducts his or her first staff meeting or the effort you have put into making a good impression with parents at back-to-school nights or open houses. As you might guess, it is equally important for literacy coaches to make good first impressions and to start off right. This chapter offers some tips for doing so.

Laying the Groundwork

It will be helpful for you to think about some things before you meet the people with whom you will be working. Some questions to ponder are as follows:

- Which of my personality strengths do I want the staff to see from the start?
- How do I want my role to be understood? For instance, do I want to be seen as a change agent, support system, or resource? (If your response is "all of the above," then you might choose to prioritize these roles.)
- What is the likeliest negative response I might initially receive from staff members, and what can I do to prepare for it?
- How can I describe my literacy coaching duties in a few words?
- How do I want to spend my first and second weeks on the job?

Your responses to these questions can help you in thinking about the manner in which you might introduce yourself to staff members individually as well as in a group. In addition, they will help you develop language that you can use in explaining your work to others, and they may indicate some trouble spots for which you can already begin preparing.

Meeting the Principal

Sit down with the principal as early as possible and definitely *before* you meet the staff as a group. Prepare notes on the points you want to be sure to make and the issues you want to explore with him or her. I recommend that the list include the following items:

- The job description—review it or plan for developing one if none exists
- Visions of literacy coaching—yours and the principal's
- History of coaching, professional development, and literacy instruction at the school (if you or the principal are new to the school)
- Your background and beliefs (be brief—support your comments with your resumé or philosophy statement)
- Communications with the principal—how often and in what format (make sure he or she knows that you want to keep him or her informed and involved)
- First steps for meeting staff, students, and parents
- Priorities for the start of the year
- Your plans for individual and small-group meetings
- Resources available (time, money, staff)
- Next meeting time, location, and topics (At this second meeting, you may want to discuss data on student reading achievement that are available and additional data that might be collected.)

Try to avoid gossiping about the staff or appearing interested in working with the principal to manipulate the staff. Demonstrate that you are professional in all aspects of the work you do.

Meeting the Staff

What does the staff want to learn from you when you first meet them? No doubt, some people are thrilled that you are there and can't wait to hear when you'll be available to assist them either inside or outside their classrooms. I'll call these the Ready-to-Go Group. On the other end of the spectrum, other people probably dread your presence in the building and are attempting to determine how to avoid you or convince you to go somewhere else. I'll call these the Put-on-the-Brakes Group. And the rest of the staff will be someplace in between, perhaps feeling curiosity, cautious enthusiasm, or restricted skepticism. I'll call these the Wait-and-See Group. The characteristics of these groups are outlined in Table 2.

I'd suggest that many new literacy coaches make the mistake of focusing on one of the groups at either end of the spectrum. Some literacy coaches put their attention on the best-case scenario and speak to the entire staff as if they are ready to jump in and work together to create major changes. These literacy coaches sometimes demonstrate their affiliation with the Ready-to-Go Group by referring to accomplishments already achieved by this group that the coaches hope to build on. This is a mistake, because the Wait-and-See Group will become more cautious and the Put-on-the-Brakes Group will become defensive and perhaps angry. Literacy coaches who focus on the individuals or aims of the Ready-to-Go Group make the rest of the staff wary that the coaches already have decided what the staff needs and who the "good" teachers are. This inhibits the staff members' openness to the literacy coaches.

Another danger of focusing on the Ready-to-Go Group is that literacy coaches probably will convey a level of enthusiasm that others on the staff don't feel. If literacy coaches are thinking about the teachers they think are doing the most exciting things in the school, the coaches will talk to the staff excitedly about the prospects for what can happen. Now, I'm not recommending a *lack* of enthusiasm. However, again, an abundance of enthusiasm may make the cautious or resistant members of the staff feel even more hesitant.

On the other hand, new literacy coaches sometimes focus on the Put-on-the-Brakes Group. When this happens, the literacy coaches make the exact opposite mistake from those who focus on the Ready-to-Go Group. Whereas the content of the discussion when focused on the Ready-to-Go Group may be about the changes taking place and soon to take place, the content of the discussion when focused on the Put-on-the-Brakes Group may be both the need to move slowly and the literacy coaches' interest in making everyone feel at ease. In the latter situation, a well-intentioned literacy coach wants even the most hesitant or resistant staff members to feel comfortable, so he or she conveys that he or she is there to do nothing that will be threatening. In the process, the staff may come to believe that the literacy coach is there to support the status quo, perhaps even to make the status quo easier to live with. This will make the literacy coach seem inconsistent or insincere if he or she proposes changes at a later point. Likewise, while the literacy coaches who focus on the Ready-to-Go Group

Table 2
Staff Groups Encountered by New Literacy Coaches

• • •

Group	Characteristics	Challenges to Coaching	Tips for Working With This Group*
Ready-to-Go Group	• Eager to try new things • Enjoy working with colleagues • Confident—not afraid to talk and ask about what they want to learn • 10–20% of staff	• Can easily captivate all of the literacy coach's time • May tempt the literacy coach to focus too much on them because they are pleasant to work with • Might intimidate coaches who lack confidence	• Give them the same amount of attention as other groups. • Leverage this group's enthusiasm by asking them to help you try out practices new to you. • Use teachers in this group as examples some of the time but not too often. • Encourage members of this group to share their knowledge and skill with teachers in other schools.
Wait-and-See Group	• Eager to improve but cautious about changes • Looking for quick signs of success (e.g., "OK, show me") • May seek clarifications about roles and expectations • 60–80% of staff	• May be thinking about past initiatives and wondering how literacy coaching is different • May feel hesitant to stand out from the group in their teaching practices or environment • May be overwhelmed by day-to-day concerns that prevent them from volunteering for new initiatives	• "Lead with the need": Identify and address immediate needs of these teachers to yield speedy results. • Listen to and learn about past efforts of these teachers; seek to identify ways that literacy coaching should be different. Ask the teachers for help. • Encourage teachers to work in pairs so they are not trying new things on their own.

(continued)

Table 2 (continued)
Staff Groups Encountered by New Literacy Coaches

● ● ●

Group	Characteristics	Challenges to Coaching	Tips for Working With This Group*
Put-on-the-Brakes Group	● Want nothing to do with the literacy coach ● Feel satisfied with their work as it is, or so dissatisfied that they don't want anyone to know ● Usually have a history of resisting initiatives ● 10–20% of staff	● Often exert influence over colleagues that discourages colleagues from participating in literacy coaching ● May be quite vocal ● May be intimidating to the literacy coach	● Do not avoid these teachers. ● Do not give these teachers undue time or mental energy. ● Support these teachers in an honest and authentic manner. ● Listen to and learn about past experiences and current beliefs and practices of these teachers. ● Take your time, but don't give up.

*Additional ideas for working with different kinds of teachers are found in this and subsequent chapters.

may convey too much enthusiasm, the coaches who focus on the Put-on-the-Brakes Group may convey negativity. They may unintentionally communicate an awareness that they can't expect too much from the staff. Then again, they also may convey fear and hesitation. These messages can become self-fulfilling prophecies. Moreover, literacy coaches who focus too much on the Put-on-the-Brakes Group may find themselves inadvertently placing their attention on the staff members who least want to work with them. (See chapter 8 for more on dealing with teachers who are resistant.)

So, what tone would I suggest for literacy coaches meeting the staff for the first time? As you may have guessed, I advocate a middle-of-the road approach. I think literacy coaches will make the most productive impressions if they honor the range of perspectives and practices that exist within most staffs. These literacy coaches will wisely avoid acknowledging particular practices or perspectives as the ones they find most exciting to work with. In addition, they will demonstrate enthusiasm for meeting the staff and interest in getting to know them but avoid overwhelming the hesitant staff members with the strength of their introductory comments.

For example, let's say that a literacy coach is introducing him- or herself to the staff at the first faculty meeting in August. Here's a message that may be productive:

> Hi. I'd like to give you a sense of who I am and what I'm doing here. I'll give you all a copy of my job description but, in a nutshell, I'm here to help you help your students achieve in literacy and beyond. I'll soon be meeting with you as individuals and grade-level teams in order to discuss what that might look like in your particular instance. Meanwhile, what I want to say is that, while I'm an expert at some things, I know you are, too. I hope we can work together to share one anothers' expertise. I believe my first job is to listen and learn— to get to know you, your interests, and your concerns. I believe we're all working for the success of the children at this school, and I look forward to being part of that effort.

An introduction such as this establishes that you want to focus on student success, you are not the only expert in the room, you want to get to know the staff before you draw any conclusions, and that you have a sense of what you're about.

I encourage literacy coaches to think of their first interactions with the school staff as the foundation for future work together. Although poor starts can be repaired, strong starts give literacy coaches the advantage of making the staff excited about working with them. From this strong base, literacy coaches can then begin to work with individuals and small groups on the staff.

Meeting Individuals and Small Groups

I would encourage you to formally meet with individual staff members or in grade-level teams as soon as possible. You may be wondering which is better, individual or small-group meetings, and unfortunately, I can't say for sure. I'd encourage you to think about the dynamics of the staff with which you are working as well as your own skills and time. It probably is ideal to meet both with groups and individuals early in the school year, but if that is not possible, you may want to consider the advantages and disadvantages in Table 3. I provide this table because it will help you decide how to meet teachers at the start of the year. However, the same information is useful as you're doing your work throughout the year. Therefore,

Table 3
Individual or Small-Group Introductions

• • •

Individual Introductions

Advantages	Disadvantages
● You have more time to listen to each person. ● An individual staff member may tell you something that he or she would not be comfortable sharing in a group. ● You and the staff member have a greater opportunity to get to know each other as individuals. ● The meetings are fairly easy to schedule because you only have to coordinate two schedules, yours and that of the staff member.	● Some individuals are more comfortable voicing potentially controversial perspectives if they know there are others in the group who share their views. ● You don't have the contributions of additional perspectives, which is especially desirable if the individual with whom you are meeting is very negative or narrowly focused. ● Individual meetings with all staff members take more time on your part.

Small-Group Introductions

Advantages	Disadvantages
● If held with grade-level teachers, including specialists and resource teachers, such meetings can build a sense of community. ● You can get a sense for how the teams do or don't work together in instructional planning. ● Members of the team will learn how their colleagues feel about important matters. ● Individuals who prefer not to speak up in a whole-staff meeting may feel comfortable speaking up at a small-group meeting and, therefore, will be heard by some of their colleagues. ● Having a few small-group meetings takes less of your time than having individual meetings with all staff members.	● One or two vocal participants can dominate the discussion. ● A literacy coach without strong group facilitation skills might feel overwhelmed by a highly vocal small group. ● Small-group meetings often are difficult to schedule because they require a shared planning time or a time outside the regular school day when all group members can meet.

refer back to it as you read chapters 6 and 7 on coaching individuals and groups, respectively.

You might ask your principal for advice, or go to the staff and ask how they prefer to meet you initially. No matter which approach you use at the start of the year, include both individual and small-group meetings in your literacy coaching duties as the year continues.

The First Interaction. The first face-to-face meeting with teachers, either individually or in small groups, often is the point when literacy coaches damage their positive first impressions. Here are some common mistakes to avoid:

- In a grade-level meeting, the literacy coach asks the teachers what they'd like to do differently. The coach is met with silence.
- At the beginning of a conversation with a teacher, the literacy coach outlines possible things he or she can do for the teacher—demonstration lessons, class observations, and instructional coplanning. The teacher says, "Thanks, but I don't need any help right now."
- The literacy coach places a sign-up sheet in the office, listing the times when he or she is available to observe in classrooms. The sheet remains blank for several weeks.

These scenarios represent unintended blunders on the part of well-intentioned literacy coaches. What happens in each scenario is that the literacy coach makes an assumption about the teachers with whom he or she is working, and the teachers deliver a clear message that the assumption is wrong: They don't want to do things differently, they don't want the literacy coach's offer of help, and they definitely don't want to be observed in their classrooms by the literacy coach.

I don't want to stereotype *all* teachers with these scenarios. In most schools, there will be a couple teachers who find such offers of help appealing, but most teachers won't. This seems to be just a reflection of human nature. After all, who wants to volunteer when someone shows up to provide unsolicited assistance? This approach to literacy coaching is sort of like selling merchandise door to door: The literacy coach shows up and tries to "get a foot in the door" by "making an offer you can't refuse." Most people are pretty wary of such offers.

There are other reasons, too, why teachers may want to avoid the literacy coach's offer of help. Teaching is a profession about which everyone has an opinion, and teachers are routinely being told what they should do. In addition, teachers often have felt powerless in their schools. Teaching is a gendered profession, meaning that it has been highly influenced by traditional perceptions of male and female roles. In the case of teaching, perceptions of appropriate female behavior can still be found in assumptions about appropriate teacher behavior, despite the great number of males who are also in the profession (Biklen, 1995). One of the characteristics of such a profession is that its members are vulnerable to being told what to do by others. Moreover, teaching is notorious for being a profession in which individuals do their work in the isolation of their classrooms (despite the fact that there are 25 or 30 students there) and in which they like to be left alone.

So what should a literacy coach do? Frame the work ahead in terms of what teachers want to do for their students. In this way, a teacher doesn't feel singled out as in need of being "fixed." Rather, the teacher and literacy coach focus on how to help the students. Here's the start-up question that works well for me:

> When you think about the kind of reading and writing you want your students to do, the kind of literate lives you want students to have, the kind of classroom you want to have, the kind of teaching you want to be able to do, what gets in your way?

I think this question (which I'll refer to as The Question from this point on) works because it avoids any implication that something is wrong with the teacher. In addition, while it does make an assumption, it makes one that is virtually always accurate: Teachers want their students to succeed and have an idea of what kind of learning and teaching will lead to that success. Various teachers may disagree about what those paths to success are or how they can gauge success, but they do want students to succeed. In addition, The Question focuses on the limitations to success "out there," not within the teacher. You might think this is naïve (e.g., what if the teacher needs to change?), but I'd suggest it is the only way you can develop trust and is an excellent way to start a conversation with a teacher. A statement that sums up this concept of acceptance before change is a well-known quote usually attributed to Carl Rogers: "The curious paradox is that when I accept myself just as I am, then I can change."

Meeting Students

Literacy coaches frequently are in classrooms, so it is important that the students get to know them. I'd encourage you to ask each classroom teacher for permission to read a book to his or her students in the first two weeks of the school year. By doing this, you will accomplish several things: First, the students will become familiar with you. This process will be helped if you say a few words about who you are and why you are working in the school before you read to the students. Second, you will provide one more reading experience for students. Third, you will get a feel for each class. Fourth, you will let the teachers get a feel for you. Finally, you will be of service at the start of the year before your more intense coaching duties may have begun. The odds are that some teachers will not have time to meet with you for any serious work in the first week or two of the school year anyway.

I'd encourage you to make yourself visible and accessible to students throughout the school year as well. Attend assemblies, visit the lunchroom, and show an interest in the students. One strategy that has worked for me is to tell the students when I introduce myself that I would like to share a secret signal they can use to indicate that they've been reading. I tell them it will be the thumbs-up signal, and when I see them in the hall or elsewhere, if they have been reading, they can quietly give me this signal. I make sure to make the signal back to the students as well. In this way, I communicate the expectation that reading is something that is a frequent activity and something to be proud of. This signal also gives the students a way to greet me without causing a lot of noise. Of course, this practice would probably seem silly to middle school students. As an alternative, you might merely engage middle school readers in informal conversations about what they've been reading. To create such conversations, you might routinely chat with students in the lunchroom or hallways. Carrying an interesting book that appeals to middle school students is a good way to begin such discussions.

Literacy coaches are typically very comfortable interacting with students. However, as they become busy working with teachers, they may struggle to find time to interact meaningfully with children. Moreover, if the coach is new to the building, the students may not recognize the literacy coach when they see her. By introducing herself to students at the beginning, the literacy coach begins to get to know the students and starts to develop routines that will enable ongoing interaction throughout the school year.

Meeting the Parents

As you plan the start of your literacy coaching duties at a new site, include plans for meeting students' parents. You may think of this as a lower priority task; however, literacy coaches need parents' support, and they have expertise to share with parents. Moreover, a growing body of research is demonstrating the value of bridging children's home and school literacies (see Appendix B for more information). If you as a literacy coach want to support such an effort, you will be wise to get to know the parents at your school and the literacies they possess.

There are easy ways to introduce yourself to parents, such as a note in a school newsletter or an appearance at a Parent–Teacher Association meeting. I'd encourage you to go beyond these steps, though, to create opportunities for *meaningful* interaction with as many parents as possible. For example, offer evening Read-a-Thons for all families. Have families rotate to four stations over a two-hour period. These stations might include a Guest Reader station (featuring the principal, the mayor, area sport figures, and local celebrities), a Silent Reading station (to which families can bring pillows, sleeping bags, and stuffed animals to make it a cozy experience), a Film station (featuring a film based on a popular children's book), and a Buddy Reading station (at which kids read with each other and the adults have a short session with you).

Another way to introduce yourself to parents is to arrange a special reading-related program for each grade level. Include the students in the program, and provide a motivation for them to get their parents to the event, which could be scheduled during the school day or in the evening. The event might include opportunities for students to read their own writing to their parents or to perform a play based on a book they have read. Those in attendance might receive a take-home writing kit or engage in a make-your-own-bookmark art activity. When the event includes students and enables them to have fun, they are motivated to attend and will encourage their parents to be there.

These are just a few ideas for making yourself visible and accessible to parents. Wise coaches will develop two or three strategies that they'll regularly use to make themselves visible and accessible to parents.

If You Previously Have Been Part of the Staff

Special challenges face literacy coaches who previously have been a part of the staff. Typically, when this occurs, the literacy coaches were classroom teachers until the point when they became coaches. The challenges accompanying this change are rooted in the reality that, if you've been teaching in the school, you've probably established affiliations with some staff members but not others, and you've probably provided the staff with at least some idea of what you believe about literacy, teaching, and learning. These are not bad things to do. Whether you are a literacy coach or a classroom teacher, you are entitled to have close colleagues and to have beliefs and preferences. However, as a new literacy coach who has previously taught at the same school, you are not really "new." In other words, many staff members probably have formed opinions of you already.

My best advice is to be consistent and honest. As far as consistency goes, continue to be the person you have been. Don't suddenly change your views or become cool to your on-staff friends. This will lead to distrust for you among many staff members. As for honesty, speak up when you are in a situation where you have previously voiced an opinion other than the group's or other than the one you now must consider as a literacy coach and instructional leader.

For example, let's say that you've been vocal about the need for students to have access to materials that are not leveled when they are reading for pleasure, inquiry, or in the content areas. (This is in opposition to a growing trend in thinking that students should always read at what is perceived to be their grade level.) If the staff is discussing the value and use of leveled books, don't pretend to be neutral on the subject. Instead, acknowledge your previously aired views and then affirm your interest in hearing and considering others' views as well. You might say the following:

> As many of you know, I've been vocal in my support of children reading non-leveled books during parts of the day. I know that some of you agree with that position and some of you don't. My job now is not to make sure that my viewpoint wins but to make sure that we use an effective process for dealing with this disagreement. I promise to do my best to be a fair leader and consider all perspectives on this issue.

Then—do exactly what you said!

Repairing a Poor Start

Don't panic if you already have started your literacy coaching job and you have not had a smooth beginning. Some Buddhist teachers say, "Everything is workable," and I think that applies here. You can still apply the ideas in this book. However, if they contradict what you've said or done previously, you need to be open about that discrepancy. Admit that you started out thinking differently and have decided that a different approach might be better.

It can be difficult to admit you've made mistakes, and it can be humbling to ask your colleagues to give you another try. But think about it: Your job will only get more difficult if you continue down a path that is ineffective. In addition, mature individuals on the staff will respect you for your willingness to reflect upon your actions and to continue growing. In fact, isn't that what you are hoping the teachers will do themselves?

Conclusion

A good start will serve you well as a literacy coach. It will help you establish yourself as a positive, likeable, and trustworthy individual. Moreover, it will give others a sense of why you are there and what you hope to do in your job. It is an investment in the rest of the school year (or beyond) because it gives you a solid starting point of mutual respect and openness, as well as a sense of direction. This strong start, like all work of literacy coaches, requires strong personal qualities. The following chapter will help you to understand and enhance such qualities.

ADDITIONAL RESOURCES FOR LITERACY COACHES

Hallowell, E.M. (1999). *Connect: 12 vital ties that open your heart, lengthen your life, and deepen your soul*. New York: Pocket Books.

Zebrowitz, L.A. (1997). *Reading faces: Window to the soul?* Boulder, CO: Westview Press.

CHAPTER 4

What Are the Qualities of an Effective Literacy Coach?

- How do I know if I have what it takes to be a literacy coach?
- Why won't teachers learn what I think they need to learn in order to do a good job?
- How can I become expert enough to do this job?
- Why do some teachers seem to resent me when I'm trying so hard to respect them?
- How can I get teachers to trust me?

Several chapters in this book address various skills of literacy coaching, such as listening, facilitating, and communicating. Before addressing these skills, though, let's talk about literacy coaches' qualities. The distinction I am making here is between a behavior that coaches use to accomplish certain tasks in certain situations—that is, a skill—and a characteristic that coaches carry with them at all times and regularly demonstrate across all situations.

The qualities that I believe to be essential to effective literacy coaching are those that lead to trust. Literacy coaches—and those with whom they work—generally acknowledge that there needs to be trust in a coaching relationship. However, literacy coaches don't always understand the significance of that need, nor do they always understand how easily a trusting coaching relationship can be undone. In this chapter, I want to examine the importance of coaching relationships and trust, and then I want to give you some tips for building and maintaining these qualities in your literacy coaching work.

It's Hardly Ever About Knowledge

Let me begin this section by telling you a story of my own coaching blunders. When I took on my first teacher leadership position, which included coach-like duties, I was one year out of graduate school. I had a master's degree in reading education, and I was confident in and proud of my new knowledge. My approach to the teachers with whom I was working reflected an unvoiced and unacknowledged (even to myself) belief that went something like this: *If these teachers only knew what I know, then they'd be the kind of good teacher that I am.*

I'm embarrassed to see the words I just wrote. It seems so disrespectful of the teachers with whom I was working, who probably had 250 combined years of teaching experience. However, in all honesty, it is what I believed. Needless to say, I didn't fare well in the coaching aspect of my job, although I must say that the teachers were quite kind to me in the manner in which they tolerated or ignored me.

I have found since then that the mistake I made is made by many literacy coaches. We think that the issue is knowledge, but it isn't. If knowledge were the essential component to behavior change, then we'd all be very different. For instance, we'd all be slender. After all, we have knowledge that weight loss will result if we burn more calories than we consume. And we'd never speed on the highway, given that we know the speed limit and know the increased danger that speeding causes. I'm not claiming that knowledge doesn't matter—of course it does to some extent—but knowledge alone does not lead to change.

You're probably nodding your head in agreement. Most educators understand the importance of attitudes, beliefs, and perceptions in assisting learners to learn; in other words, educators recognize that attitudes, beliefs, and perceptions can interfere with learners' abilities to acquire new knowledge. But that's not what I'm referring to here. I'm not saying that we have to consider attitudes, beliefs, and perceptions in order to help teachers put new knowledge to best use. I'm saying that the issue is *rarely about knowledge in the first place.* Consider the following examples:

● Bob teaches fifth grade and never reads aloud to his class. He knows how to read aloud, and he has been told at workshops led by his district curriculum coordinator that reading aloud is a recommended instructional strategy for all elementary school teachers. However, Bob believes that it is a waste of time to read to fifth graders and that the kids would feel insulted if he read to them.

● Melinda is a kindergarten teacher. She has read the summary of the National Reading Panel (NRP) report (National Institute of Child Health and Human Development, 2000)—which recommends direct, systematic instruction in phonics for kindergarten teachers—and she knows that the NRP based its recommendation on a meta-analysis of research. However, Melinda has observed that some children in her classroom enter school with strong phonics knowledge because they have had frequent reading experiences at home, so she tries to replicate those home reading experiences, instead of using the suggested phonics workbook. In addition, she finds teacher-generated research to be more useful than meta-analyses of experimental or quasi-experimental studies, so she pays little attention to the NRP recommendations.

● Sally's first-grade students are supposed to read for at least 15 minutes each evening, and an adult is to sign a form each week to indicate that this reading has been done. Sally knows that one of her students, Michael, spends his evenings with his grandmother while his mother works. Sally knows that the grandmother is fluent in reading and writing Spanish, but not English. Michael indicates that he reads for more than 15 minutes each evening, and his knowledge of books would support this claim. However, he never returns the form because his grandmother cannot read it. Sally knows this is not Michael's fault, but she believes every child must be treated in the same manner and, therefore, gives him a "needs improvement" mark on his report card for the item "Completes Assignments." Also, when it is time for the quarterly movie and pizza party for those who have returned a signed form every week, Michael is excluded.

In each of these situations, knowledge is not the factor in the teacher's decision making. Rather, Bob's perceptions of middle school, Melinda's opinions about phonics learning and research, and Sally's value that all should be treated the same lead to the action each educator takes.

Ironically, the preparation that most literacy coaches receive is in the knowledge domain. Currently, literacy coaches are taught about the five elements of instruction recommended by the NRP, the components of a strong reading curriculum, and, perhaps, the characteristics of effective professional development workshops. I think this kind of knowledge is excellent for literacy coaches to have, and I would not hire a coach who didn't have it. However, I find that knowledge is to coaching like a car is to driving. It's what propels the activity forward, but it won't happen successfully unless the person behind the wheel is skilled in steering it. A literacy coach who knows a great deal about literacy instruction but cannot develop relationships, build trust, and work with the non–knowledge-related issues of teaching will fail.

The remaining sections of this chapter provide suggestions for accomplishing these essential tasks.

You're Not the Expert

New literacy coaches or those exploring the possibility of becoming literacy coaches often express to me their self-doubts, indicating that they don't think they know everything they need to know in order to help teachers. (Again, issues of knowledge are at the forefront.) These individuals express concerns that they don't have as much teaching experience as the teachers with whom they might work, that they can't keep up with all of the professional literature, or that they can't demonstrate expertise in all grade levels. In other words, they think they need to be content experts in order to be good literacy coaches.

The notion of being an expert sets up literacy coaches for failure because no one can be an expert on all aspects of literacy teaching and at all grade levels. Moreover, even if literacy coaches were experts in all those areas, it would be impossible for them to be experts on any particular teaching dilemma because such teaching dilemmas involve the students in a teacher's classroom. Any group of students brings with it a unique set of characteristics, strengths, and challenges, plus a unique alchemy among the students themselves. Therefore, there is no way that literacy coaches could be experts on the students in every classroom.

Some literacy coaches are indeed experts, but only within a certain range of grades or on specific topics such as guided reading, writing workshop, or running record assessment. The people who have an easier time literacy coaching are probably generalists—They know some things about most aspects of literacy teaching across a range of grade levels, but they are by no means experts in all those things.

Trying to be the expert is damaging because, beyond trying to do the impossible, it interferes with the development of a trusting relationship with teachers. If literacy coaches present themselves as experts, teachers will respond either by believing or not believing that claim. Either response leads to problems for the coach, as described below:

Teachers see the literacy coach as an expert. If the teachers do believe the literacy coach is an expert, then the literacy coach will fail to live up to their expectations because, again, no individual can be an expert on all aspects of teaching at all grade levels and with all groups of students. Meanwhile, the teachers who turn to the literacy coach as expert often fail to acknowledge their own expertise. In addition, believing in the literacy coach as an expert creates a sense that there is a discrete set of information (which brings us back to the knowledge myth again) essential for teaching successfully, and that the task is for the teachers to take in that knowledge and make it their own. Such a notion obscures the fact that good teachers are problem finders and problem solvers, not possessors of all the expert knowledge that they will ever need.

Teachers dispute the literacy coach's efforts to appear to be an expert. On the other hand, some teachers will not believe that the literacy coach is an expert. If the literacy coach maintains the stance of expert and teachers doubt him, communication will become a power struggle, with all the individuals involved trying to prove that they are right. Moreover, there is a risk that the teachers who doubt the literacy coach's expertise will note every time the literacy coach is not all-knowing and they may bring these moments to everyone's attention to gain power over the coach and/or the situation. Here's an example.

● ● ● ● ●

Betty and Beatrice, sixth-grade teachers, are sure that their literacy coach, Jorge, is not the expert he claims to be. When at a faculty meeting he incorrectly states that the sixth-grade spelling lists are not correlated to the content areas, Betty and Beatrice exchange looks across the room. A week later, Betty asks Jorge about the latest research on writing revision, and Jorge stammers. Betty tells Beatrice about this at lunchtime and they both note this failure on Jorge's part for future use. Finally, at a staff meeting to discuss a new writing program, Jorge inaccurately describes the state-mandated writing assessment. Beatrice uses this opportunity to prove that Jorge is not an expert: She raises her hand and begins explaining why she doesn't think the program, which Jorge is advocating for, is a good idea. In the process, she points out Jorge's inaccurate claims about the state test and hints that he has not learned about the current sixth-grade program well enough. She also cites some research on writing instruction that contradicts Jorge's stammering response to Betty a few weeks earlier. Jorge looks uninformed, and his position as advocate for the writing program is undermined considerably. Betty and Beatrice have used their previous insights about his lack of expertise against him.

Some new literacy coaches worry that a nonexpert approach will backfire because it will lead teachers to assume that the literacy coaches know nothing and can't help the teachers. To avoid this situation, you might want to practice a short explanation of how you see your role and the role of the teacher. When I'm getting to know teachers in a literacy coaching situation, I usually say something such as,

> I don't approach this job as an expert. Although I know some things, I also know that you know some things. We are all experts to an extent, and what I hope to do is provide an opportunity for you to share and build on your

expertise. In the process, I'll share some of the things I know, but I want you to share your expertise with me as well.

The goal is to make clear that your literacy coaching task is not about telling the teachers what you know and expecting them to accept it without question. Rather, the message should be that coaching is about relationships, sharing, and mutual respect for the purpose of helping one another to grow.

True Respect

Educators frequently talk about respect—we respect each other, we respect our students, and we respect administrators. Coaches express the same desire to be respectful. Literacy coaches express the same desire to be respectful. In my experience, though, what's referred to as respect often means being friendly and polite while manipulating others into doing what you want them to do.

For example, Meg, a literacy coach in an elementary school, wants teachers to provide more strategic instruction in reading comprehension. However, in her school she sees teachers assigning many activities in which students are asked to respond to what was read but are not helped to develop strategies for understanding. She wants the teachers at her school to provide instruction and practice in reading comprehension strategies, but she wants to be respectful. Here's her plan:

● ● ● ● ●

Meg knows that Kevin, a second-grade teacher, is successfully providing strategy instruction for reading comprehension, so she highlights his teaching at an after-school workshop. Then, when conferencing with Melinda, the other second-grade teacher, Meg offers to cover Melinda's class for a morning so Melinda can observe Kevin's strategy instruction. Meanwhile, Meg approaches the fourth-grade teachers, Patrice and LaWanda. They have taught together for 10 years and have established parallel routines. However, Meg and LaWanda are both interested in quilting, and Meg has used that opportunity to get to know LaWanda better. She learns that LaWanda has been wanting to do an integrated unit with quilts as the theme, but Patrice is not interested. Meg suggests that she'll work with LaWanda on such a unit, and LaWanda agrees. Meg doesn't mention it to LaWanda, but she intends to incorporate reading comprehension strategy instruction into the unit. Meg has fewer ideas for how to approach the teachers in first and fifth grade, so she begins in a low-key manner by placing articles from The Reading Teacher in their mailboxes once a week, with a note that she'd be glad to talk about them if the teachers are interested. On the other hand, Meg knows that the teachers in grade three, Holly and Chandra, are not providing the kind of instruction Meg recommends. In fact, they have openly resisted her suggestions and have failed to attend the last two after-school workshops that Meg has led. Therefore, Meg decides not to waste time on Holly and Chandra. Rather, she focuses on the teachers she believes she can move along most easily.

If asked, Meg would assure an observer unequivocally that she is respecting the teachers. She would say that she is focusing on Kevin's success and enabling Melinda to have the opportunity to experience the same success. She would suggest that she is capitalizing on LaWanda's own interest, and that her low-key approach to the teachers in the first and fifth grades is nonthreatening and not forcing them to change. As for Holly and Chandra, Meg would say that she is showing respect to them and the entire school by not causing trouble.

I feel a bit unkind suggesting Meg isn't being as respectful as she might be. Like many real-life literacy coaches, this imaginary literacy coach is trying her best to implement her notion of what respect looks and sounds like. Unfortunately, respect is one of those virtues that we all strive to practice but rarely discuss or get assistance in practicing. So let's look at various examples of respect:

- There's the "respect" that junior high school kids want, which means, "You, the adult, are respecting me when you let me do whatever I want and then pick up the pieces when I make a mistake."
- There's the "respect" of an unhappily married couple, in which both partners loathe some of the other's habits but remain silent out of respect for the sanctity of the marriage.
- There's the "respect" of the doctor who fails to address her heart patient's smoking habits because she knows it will upset the patient.
- There's the "respect" of a police officer who politely tells a driver to have a good day after giving her a $78 speeding citation.
- There's the "respect" of an office worker who wants the desk near the window and, therefore, begins to tell her colleague, who has the window desk, about the harmful effects of the sun's rays.

These might seem like dubious examples of respect, but in some ways they parallel the respect that Meg is showing to the teachers in her fictitious school. Meg is deciding what is best for the teachers with whom she works and then developing strategies to get them to do what she wants. These strategies include the subtle manipulation of placing journal articles in mailboxes, encroaching on a 10-year teaching partnership when she sees an opportunity, and dismissing those teachers who don't agree with her. Her subtle manipulation is aimed at meeting her goals without considering the teachers' goals. I would suggest that this is not true respect.

I also would suggest that these approaches leave teachers feeling uncomfortable. Meg is naïve if she thinks the teachers she works with aren't aware at some level that they are being manipulated. Most adults can sense when they are being manipulated, and none of us likes to feel this way. In fact, such a feeling reduces trust and is detrimental to relationships. In a truly respectful relationship, the parties involved strive for a balance between being themselves as much as possible and honoring the needs of the other to be as much themselves as possible. This occurs while maintaining the function of the relationship, such as supporting a marriage, meeting work goals, or keeping one's body healthy.

Table 4 demonstrates what respect in a literacy coaching relationship might look and sound like. As you can see, this approach is one in which the literacy coach is a listener and learner first. The purpose of this attentiveness to the teacher is to truly learn about the teacher and the work he or she is doing. The literacy coach listens carefully and asks carefully worded questions that indicate that the literacy coach is there to help the teacher meet his or her goals, not the other way around. In such a truly respectful relationship, the teacher and literacy coach may not agree, but they have enough trust that they can express their goals, beliefs, and values without worrying that the other person will either dismiss them or manipulate them.

Myles Horton, founder of the famous Highlander Folk School, expressed this concept by saying that a good education includes "respect for people's abilities to learn and to act and to shape their own lives" (Horton & Freire, 1990, p. 177). Just as Horton and his colleagues applied this concept to their education of adults (including Rosa Parks) seeking social change in the mid-1900s, so can literacy coaches seeking educational change apply this concept of respect to their work. Literacy coaches do so when they recognize that teachers need to act and shape their own work lives. Respectful literacy coaches ask good questions, provide resources, make suggestions, assist in problem finding and solving, demonstrate instructional strategies, and engage in other activities to influence teachers' changes, but with an emphasis on the *teachers'* goals. On the other hand,

Table 4
What Respectful Literacy Coaching Relationships Look and Sound Like

• • •

Objective	Looks Like	Sounds Like
Planning for coaching	The literacy coach meets with teachers to listen to and learn about their concerns, strengths, needs, and efforts so far.	"When you [the teacher] think about your goals for your teaching—the kind of readers and writers you want your students to be, the kind of classroom you want to have, and the kind of work you want to do—what gets in the way?"
Altering teaching practices	The literacy coach and teacher look at data, standards, curricular goals, student characteristics, and teaching strengths and interests in order to establish priorities.	"What are you doing successfully? What do you want to do differently? How can I help?"
Improving assessment practices	The literacy coach and teacher plan for assessment when they plan for instruction and then collect meaningful data, including student work samples. Schoolwide, the staff examine and talk about a range of formal and informal assessments and what they mean for the curriculum, staff organization, and school goals.	"How will you know when your efforts have been successful? What will success look and sound like?"

(continued)

Table 4 (continued)
What Respectful Literacy Coaching Relationships
Look and Sound Like

• • •

Objective	Looks Like	Sounds Like
Organizing for instruction	The literacy coach and teacher plot the teacher's daily and weekly schedules and match teaching goals to time allocations. This process includes consideration of how multiple goals and standards can be met with particular organizational structures and ways to collaborate with other school staff members.	"Let's find the time and human resources to help you meet your goals."

literacy coaches who lack true respect focus on getting teachers to implement the *coaches'* goals.

So what do you do if a teacher has poor goals or no goals or is resistant to your support? Chapter 8 focuses entirely on these questions.

Conclusion

Essential literacy coaching qualities are those that literacy coaches demonstrate in virtually all situations and when working with all staff members. These qualities are habits of action and habits of mind that develop trust. Three essential qualities of effective coaching are

1. attention to attitudes, beliefs, and perceptions as precursors to change;

2. valuing the expertise of others and the limitations of one's own "expertise"; and

3. true respect as reflected in a commitment to helping teachers meet their goals.

ADDITIONAL RESOURCES FOR LITERACY COACHES

Anderson, G.L. (1998). Toward authentic participation: Deconstructing the discourses of participatory reforms in education. *American Educational Research Journal*, *35*(4), 571–603.

Corrie, L. (1995). The structure and culture of staff collaboration: Managing meaning and opening doors. *Educational Review*, *47*(1), 89–99.

Hallowell, E.M. (1999). *Connect: 12 vital ties that open your heart, lengthen your life, and deepen your soul*. New York: Pocket Books.

CHAPTER 5

How Can I Communicate Well With Teachers?

- What are key communication strategies for literacy coaching?

- How can I be a good listener?

- How can I be responsive to teachers without being too directive?

- How can I encourage teachers to open up to me?

A good deal of the work done by literacy coaches is verbal, and much of that work is done in conversation. Literacy coaches meet routinely with teachers, principals, teaching assistants, and parents. The discussions usually are not about the literacy coaches' own work, and when discussing others' work, the potential pitfalls are many. No one likes to feel judged, labeled, or put down. Even positive statements made by a literacy coach can be misunderstood by others, leading the receivers of the comments to wonder why the literacy coach thinks he or she is superior to them.

Wise literacy coaches develop communication skills that minimize the chances that their words will be misunderstood or misinterpreted and that maximize trust and communication between themselves and those with whom they work. This chapter provides strategies that will be useful in these endeavors. The first strategy is listening; the second strategy is silence; and the rest of the strategies are phrases that prompt further reflection and sharing on the part of teachers. You may want to make a bookmark or index card with these tips on it and attach it to your clipboard, desk, or some other place where you'll see it easily. However, good communication doesn't come from memorizing a list of strategies. These tips are only scaffolds to assist you as you practice the coaching skills of listening, mirroring, and supporting and as you discover your own words to value in your literacy coaching work.

Listening

Everyone knows how to listen, right? Everyone has ears, and almost everyone can use those ears to hear others. Listening is just a matter of paying attention to what one hears. These are of course the basics of listening, but despite the simplicity of the process, its success rate is not that high. Listening involves four stages: (1) using your senses to note what someone else says, (2) paying attention to what you hear, (3) making sense of what you hear, and (4) providing feedback so the speaker knows that he or she was heard and understood.

For instance, if your spouse tells you that he is exhausted from the day at work, and you successfully listen to him, the following processes will occur:

1. Your ears will take in not only the words, "Whew, what a day!" but also hear your spouse's tone of voice, and your eyes will notice the manner in which his mouth expels a gust of breath and the way he drops his jacket wearily on the couch.

2. You will pay attention to these things, as opposed to watching TV or talking on the phone, while your spouse does and says them.

3. You will make sense of your spouse's words and actions: He is tired because the work day has been long, difficult, or both. From the tone of voice, you know this even though he didn't actually say it. (Also note that if he had said "Whew, what a day!" but done something else, such as rub his hands together and smile broadly, you might have made different sense of his words and actions. In this latter case, perhaps he has had an exceptionally good day.)

4. You let your spouse know that you heard him by making eye contact, smiling half-heartedly, giving a backrub, or saying that perhaps supper will cheer him up.

The act of listening can break down at any of these stages. The listener's senses, attention, and brain must be engaged, and the listener must communicate back to the other person that he or she has been heard. Moreover, what I've described is just basic listening. In many cases, emotions and biases also come into play. Frequently, the listener's response to the speaker indicates misunderstanding and the parties involved must make another attempt to understand each other. Sometimes, the listener's own expectations get in the way of the sense he or she makes from what the speaker has said. These examples demonstrate the complexity of listening.

Given the primacy of listening in the work you do, seek ways to optimize your chances of listening successfully. Here are some suggestions for doing just that:

- Practice focusing on one person or activity at a time, no matter how busy you are.
- Take notes if it helps you absorb what you are hearing. However, *don't* take notes when the other person is talking about something that is highly significant to him or her. In those instances, eye contact is more important.
- Change your body language to communicate openness and attentiveness. Turn your shoulders toward the person speaking, adopt an open facial expression—with your facial muscles relaxed and your lips neither pursed nor entirely apart—and keep your eyes on the speaker much of the time, but not constantly because that would make it seem that you are staring.
- Pay attention to the responses you give in order to communicate that you have heard the speaker and attempted to understand him or her. With people you know well, or in situations that have no risk, such communication is often minimal and needs no prior consideration or even awareness. However, when you are trying to build trust with teachers whom you are coaching, you will benefit from being a bit more aware of your listening responses.
- Consider making a quick map of what you've heard and asking the other person to check it for accuracy. A map is a visual representation of ideas or of a story, using words, symbols, shapes, arrows, pictures, and anything else that helps you recall the important points.
- Ask the other speaker if you can try to paraphrase what he or she has just said so you can check that you have heard correctly.
- Adopt key phrases and terms used by the other speaker. For instance, if you usually call sustained silent reading *SSR time* but a teacher with whom you are working calls it *DEAR (Drop Everything and Read) time*, then when talking to him or her, say "DEAR time."

Listening is at the heart of all literacy coaching. Start with it and, when in doubt, return to it. Listening for further information is a tactic that will rarely fail to assist a literacy coach.

Silence

One of the most valuable tools you can have in your toolkit of coaching skills is silence. When a teacher asks a literacy coach a question or tells a literacy coach about a struggle, the coach probably will do what most humans do: attempt to answer. However, I'd encourage you to wait a moment—a count of about two seconds—before responding. This pause provides two valuable opportunities. First, it gives you the chance to breathe. A deep breath before responding can make you feel centered and calm, and you will be more likely to provide an effective response from that position. Second, the pause gives the other person another chance to say more. You'll be surprised to find that the other person frequently does use this time to provide more information and, in fact, it is often information that is highly valuable.

Think about it: When we prepare to share a problem with someone else, we often think it through logically and prepare an exact statement or step-by-step explanation of what we are struggling with. This prepared information is what comes out in the initial statement or question. When given another second, though, we often tell how we feel or add a less thought-out but still important piece of information. Here are two examples:

Example 1

Teacher: I just don't know what to do with Justin and Marissa. They are both reading much more difficult material than their classmates, and I don't see anything they need from me.

[The literacy coach waits in silence.]

Teacher: I feel so useless!

Example 2

Teacher: What can I do about kids who don't want to revise their writing?

[The literacy coach waits in silence.]

Teacher: I've tried using peer revision, but that doesn't work. I've also tried having conferences with each child, but I can't find the time!

In Example 1, the extra moment allows the teacher to share a feeling that reveals self-doubt. That may be the underlying issue for the teacher, and if the literacy coach had jumped in without waiting, the coach might have offered a lot of knowledge-based information about the needs of highly successful readers, when what the teacher really needed was a response to her feelings that she can't help the stronger students. Of course, the statement "I feel so useless" also could just be an off-the-cuff remark. An effective literacy coach would gather more information to determine whether the teacher needed ideas for helping strong readers, bolstering of her sense of efficacy, both, or neither.

In Example 2, the pause provided by the literacy coach gives the teacher time to tell more about what he has tried in the classroom. The teacher then offers a slight sense of why those efforts didn't work. This comment gives the literacy coach a great deal more information to build on and from which to learn more.

A moment's silence gives teachers time to elaborate further on what they are thinking or feeling. It also calms the literacy coach and helps him or her to focus.

Filler Phrases

My next suggestion is not silence, but it's not really a word, either. It's a filler phrase such as "Hmmm" or "Uh-huh." Such filler phrases tell the teacher that you are listening to him or her and that you are engaged with what he or she is saying, but, like silence, they leave space for the teacher to say more.

There are two rules for using a filler phrase: (1) Intone it in a neutral way, and (2) don't overuse it. Because a filler phrase is so short, a great deal of what is communicated by it comes from the tone of your voice. Try saying "Hmmm" aloud right now, in several ways, particularly by raising or lowering the pitch of your voice at the end. When "Hmmm" ends with a rising pitch, it sounds as though you are surprised. On the other hand, when "Hmmm" ends with a decreasing pitch, you sound like you are negatively judging. Let's look at another example, with three variations.

Example 3A

Teacher: I can't fit all the pieces of reading workshop into my day.

Literacy coach: Hmmm...[voice rising]

In this example, the literacy coach's intonation may lead the teacher to believe that the coach does not believe she is accurately describing the situation, or that the literacy coach does not understand why the teacher is unable to complete this task. The teacher may feel devalued or inferior as a result. It may seem as though the literacy coach is thinking, "I could fit it all in, why can't she?"

Example 3B

Teacher: I can't fit all the pieces of reading workshop into my day.

Literacy coach: Hmmm...[voice lowering]

In this example, the literacy coach's intonation may suggest that he is disappointed in the teacher. The teacher may feel negatively judged and could have the urge to avoid sharing honestly with the literacy coach in the future.

Example 3C

Teacher:	I can't fit all the pieces of reading workshop into my day.
Literacy coach:	Hmmm... [pitch of voice remains the same]
Teacher:	Yeah, I have specials during workshop time on Monday and Thursday. Also, guided reading seems to take so long.

In this example, where the filler phrase is presented in a neutral manner, the teacher feels comfortable sharing more. She senses that the literacy coach is listening in a nonjudgmental manner.

The second rule for using filler phrases is not to overuse them. We've probably all had a conversation with someone who says "Uh-huh" every few seconds. It leads us to wonder if the other person is impatient with us. Overusing a filler phrase has the opposite effect of what is desired: It makes the speaker feel *less* listened to. It causes self-doubt in the speaker and may lead him to shorten what he wishes to say. It also may limit the development of trust between a literacy coach and a teacher, particularly because the teacher may wonder if the literacy coach is too short on time or patience to be of help.

When used effectively, filler phrases can assure the speaker that the literacy coach is attentive to what is being said. In order to convey this message, literacy coaches need to monitor the pitch of their voices as well as the frequency with which they use fillers.

"Say Some More About That"

One of my favorite phrases is "Say some more about that." Obviously, these words encourage the other person to talk more—to elaborate upon his or her question, concern, or observation. This statement also has the same effect as silence or saying "Hmmm," in the sense that it shows that the literacy coach is listening and creates conversational space for the teacher to say more. However, it also makes explicit the fact that the literacy coach wants or needs some more information.

The effectiveness of "Say some more about that" is that it is neutral. It does not commit the speaker to any opinion and does not take the discussion in any particular direction. If, on the other hand, a more specific question or statement is made, the discussion may veer in a direction not desired by the teacher. For instance, in Example 4A, the teacher is struggling with a particular aspect of her spelling program, but the literacy coach's question does not get to the root of the matter.

Example 4A

Teacher: The kids' writing is so poor. I just don't know what to do.

Literacy coach: Have you tried using the rubric that the district language arts department has developed?

Teacher: Yes, but there is so much on the rubric. I can only focus on a little at a time, and I still have so many concerns with the writing I get from the kids.

Literacy coach: Let's talk about how you introduce the elements of the rubric to your students in your minilessons.

In this example, spelling never even comes up. The literacy coach asks a follow-up question, but it is too directive in shaping the conversation. For contrast, look at Example 4B, in which the literacy coach suggests that the teacher "say some more about that."

Example 4B

Teacher: The kids' writing is so poor. I just don't know what to do.

Literacy coach: Say some more about that.

Teacher: Well, we've been writing persuasive essays, and the kids get the idea that they are supposed to give reasons to support their claims.

Literacy coach: Um-hmmm.

Teacher: But the writing I get is so hard to read! I can't tell what the children are trying to say.

Literacy coach: Say some more, please.

Teacher: Well, some of the kids are still using invented spelling, and others just, well, they don't think spelling is important.

By asking the teacher to say more—and by using that tactic more than once—the literacy coach learns in greater detail about the teacher's concerns. The ensuing conversation will be much more focused and will be more likely to attend to the teacher's concerns.

Notice that there is sort of a continuum here: You might start with a moment's pause; then if the person doesn't say more, say "Hmmm"; and finally ask the person to say more, if more information is still needed.

However, don't get too caught up in this sequence. Use it at times, but use any one of the responses whenever you wish, as well.

"What Do You Think?"

Annette Sword-Peterson, a literacy coach in Rockford, Illinois, taught me this strategy. She has observed that often we know the answers to our own questions, if we are given enough time and are encouraged to trust ourselves. So, from Annette I've learned the usefulness of asking, "What do you think?" This question serves several purposes: It demonstrates that the literacy coach values the teacher as a problem solver and decision maker, it shows the literacy coach's belief that there is not just one expert in the room, and it gives the teacher a chance to listen to her own inner guide. These benefits can be seen in Example 5.

Example 5

Teacher:	Olivia has been reading nothing but books in the Boxcar Children series. I think it has been weeks since she has chosen anything else to read during workshop time. I'm not sure if I should let her continue or tell her she has to read something else.
Literacy coach:	What do you think?
Teacher:	Well, Olivia's running records and retellings show that she's getting good practice in using strategies when she reads those books.
	[Pause]
Teacher:	But I would like to expose her to some other authors and genres.
Literacy coach:	What could you do?
Teacher:	Well, maybe I'll show her my conference notes about how well she's doing, so she knows she's not doing anything wrong. And maybe I'll show her a couple of other book series—I know that's part of why she likes The Boxcar Children, because it's a series—and invite her to read one, but not force her.

Frequently, we know what we want to do, but we need support in discovering it and doing it. However, there are times when we really are stuck. Because literacy coaches are not mind readers, they cannot be sure which is the case with any given teacher, although there may be clues. After working with a teacher for a while, you may become aware of subtle qualities to the conversation—such as the teacher's tone of voice or facial expression—that indicate whether the teacher is asking for your ideas or needing to explore his own. As a literacy coach, you may not be even consciously aware of these signals. You may just develop a sense of when the teacher needs help and when he needs support in answering his own question or solving his own problem.

On the other hand, you may not have this sense in a particular coaching situation, perhaps because you don't know the teacher well. In such cases, there is little harm in asking, "What do you think?" You can even be explicit and say, "Sometimes I find that I'm most helpful by listening to a teacher's own ideas about how to solve a problem, and sometimes I'm most helpful when I try to solve the problem. I'm not sure which you need right now. Can you help me?" Remember, there's no need to rush to an answer. Take your time. It will be an investment in the effectiveness of your literacy coaching work.

"I Don't Know...Let's Find Out"

As I've mentioned in previous chapters, one of the greatest dangers for a literacy coach is the temptation to be the expert. Yes, you know some things and have some valuable experience, and you should share your insights freely. However, if you are unsure about something, say so. Let the teacher you are working with know if you don't know.

Saying "I don't know" can be difficult for many of us, probably because we are human and many people feel like failures if they don't know the answer. If you struggle to admit that you don't know something, you might want to practice admitting it with trusted friends, your spouse or partner, or even your children. Then you can add this phrase to your literacy coaching toolkit.

The phrase does have one benefit in and of itself, at least some of the time, because it demonstrates for the teacher your comfort with *not* having all the answers. This may make some teachers more comfortable in coming to you when they themselves are lacking information or insight. However, the phrase has additional value not for what it says but for what might happen if you *don't* use it. Without this phrase, you may muddle through a conversation by trying to "fake it," an approach that is likely to be unhelpful to the teacher and may undermine your ability to be effective in the future. (Literacy coaches who try to fake knowledge usually are trying to be experts. As we've discussed previously, this tactic always fails.)

Note, however, that the phrase doesn't end with "I don't know." If it did, you might feel ineffective, and the teacher probably would feel frustrated. When you add "Let's find out" to the phrase, you do two things. First, you remind the teacher that he or she is not alone: You, and perhaps others, can work with the teacher to solve his or her problem or answer his or her question, even if the solution or answer is not apparent at that moment. In addition, by saying "I don't know...let's find out," you demonstrate what good teaching is all about.

There is a myth in the education profession—and outside it—that a good teacher is one who has no problems. A good teacher goes into the classroom in the morning, teaches effortlessly and effectively all day, and goes home at the end of the day, only to do it all over the next day. Even though we know that *every* teacher faces problems all day long, too often we feel embarrassed by the teaching problems we ourselves face. This probably is one of the reasons why some teachers prefer to work in isolation and why teachers become extremely self-conscious when being observed teaching. It also adds to the fear felt by beginning teachers: They know they are far from having problem-free days, and they can't imagine they'll ever get to that point.

It's time that we put this myth to rest. The truth is that good teachers are problem solvers. They have a lot of problems and aren't afraid to admit it, probably because they know that one of the ways they can get solutions is by talking about problems with literacy coaches, principals, parents, other teachers, and even students. As a literacy coach, you deliver a powerful message when you demonstrate a problem-solving stance. You also help to shift the culture of a school when you take your own ignorance in stride, admit it, and ask a teacher to work with you to figure something out. This approach reminds all educators that problem solving is our business. Example 6 gives an illustration.

Example 6

Teacher:	The kids hate writing in their journals. They've been doing it for years and say they're tired of it. When I tell them it's journal time, they groan. How can I get them to like journaling?
Literacy coach:	What do you think?
Teacher:	I feel like I've tried everything. Sometimes I give a topic; sometimes I let them choose. We've brainstormed topic ideas. I've let them write with buddies. I've let them sit or lie on the rug during journal time. I'm out of ideas! What can I do?
Literacy coach:	I'm not sure. Can we work on this together to figure it out?
Teacher:	Sure, I could use the help. Where do we begin?

If you as a literacy coach don't know the solution to a problem, admit it. Then invite the teacher to work with you to solve it. This approach is sincere, helpful, and supportive of collaboration. It conveys that in education there is no one expert and that all educators can be problem solving.

Conclusion

The communication strategies presented in this chapter—listening well, maintaining silence, and putting to use a few phrases that encourage teachers to say and reflect more—can be useful to all literacy coaches. I urge you to try these strategies and observe which ones work for you. Also, develop your own tactics that are useful. As you reflect on a particular conference, presentation, or demonstration, ask yourself about the language you used and why it was or wasn't effective.

I recently heard a colleague present some of her research at a staff meeting. At one point, she recognized that the terms she was using were contradictory, and she declared, "Oh, language is such a problem!" Then she went on, using the same contradictory terms. I encourage you to do the opposite. Recognize that language sometimes can be a problem, and then become a careful observer of which terms are effective and which aren't. Having a few key phrases in your literacy coaching toolkit can make all the difference.

The tools and qualities highlighted in this chapter support literacy coaching processes. The following chapters will suggest structures for those processes, whether they take place with individual teachers or in group meetings.

ADDITIONAL RESOURCES FOR LITERACY COACHES

Dimitrius, J., & Mazzarella, M. (1999). *Reading people: How to understand people and predict their behavior—anytime, anyplace.* New York: Ballantine.

Nichols, M.P. (1995). *The lost art of listening: How learning to listen can improve relationships.* New York: Guilford.

Tannen, D. (1986). *That's not what I meant! How conversational style makes or breaks relationships.* New York: Ballantine.

CHAPTER 6

How Do I Coach Individuals?

- Should I include individual conferences in my coaching work?

- What is my role during a conference?

- How can I keep track of all of the conferences I am having?

- What should I do when a teacher repeatedly gets us off track during a conference?

I've been surprised to find that some literacy coaches do a great deal of conferring with teachers on an individual basis, while other literacy coaches don't even think about such conferences. I suspect that this discrepancy reflects the difference in the amount and kind of training literacy coaches receive, as well as differences in the definitions of literacy coaching jobs in various schools and school districts. I believe that one-on-one conferences with teachers are valuable to a literacy coach's work and should be conducted on a regular basis. This chapter explains the value of such conferences and provides tips for facilitating them.

Why Have Individual Conferences?

The value of individual conferences reflects both the nature of teaching and the nature of literacy coaching. Teaching has long been recognized as an individual activity. Despite support over the years for teacher collaboration, shared decision making, team teaching, and peer coaching, much of a teacher's work is still done in a classroom with, of course, 20–30 students there, but with no other adults in the room. Given that the teaching act is solitary, planning for teaching and developing one's teaching skills often are solitary acts as well. Again, efforts have been made by school leaders to support collaborative planning, and certainly every teacher has participated in professional development workshops with colleagues, but the task of changing one's practice and reflecting on that change often is done by the individual teacher. Therefore, it makes sense that some aspects of literacy coaching might best be done on a one-to-one basis.

The nature of literacy coaching is that it is responsive to teachers' needs and strengths and to the efforts of teachers to respond to students' needs. Although members of the teaching profession share some common characteristics—they are disproportionately female and middle class, almost all have bachelor's degrees, and nearly half have advanced degrees (National Center for Education Statistics, 2003)—they also vary a great deal. In addition, teachers' concerns vary and the focus of their professional growth varies. Moreover, even teachers with similar needs and desires for change may have very different students to whom they are responding. Therefore, if a literacy coach wants to help a teacher, the literacy coach needs to include individual conferencing as one of his or her practices. (You may want to refer to Table 3, page 44, which summarizes the advantages and disadvantages of meeting with groups or individuals.)

Scheduling Individual Conferences

I encourage literacy coaches to schedule individual conferences on a regular basis. A conference should be like an ongoing conversation. If it happens only once or if conferences are scheduled too far apart from each other, that conversation feels disjointed, if it feels like a conversation at all. Therefore, literacy coaches should schedule individual conferences once a month at a minimum. If you can establish a regular time—such as the first Monday of every month at 3:30 p.m.—then the teacher can put you into his or her schedule for the entire year and you both can count on that time being available.

If you are a literacy coach in a large school and can't regularly get to all teachers for individual conferences, then you might divide the staff into quarters. Then, you could focus on having regular conferences—weekly or every other week—with, say, kindergarten and first-grade teachers during the first quarter, second- and third-grade teachers during the second quarter, and so on. During the part of the year when a group of teachers is not having regular individual conferences with you, you probably would want to schedule one individual conference and at least one grade-level team meeting. This approach assures that a conversation is created for each teacher at some point during the year, while communication still exists the rest of the year. It is not an ideal situation—the ideal is to have regular one-on-one conferences with each teacher all year long—but it is a tolerable compromise for an overworked literacy coach.

When scheduling your individual conferences, work as best as you can with the teacher's schedule in order to make it the most convenient and least disruptive for the teacher. Schedule a 30-minute time period. If teachers are guaranteed a duty-free lunch period, do your best not to use that time for literacy coaching conferences. If the teacher (or the literacy coach) doesn't have 30 minutes available on a given day, push for another day when both of you will. (I find that if I'm rushed, I'm much less effective as a literacy coach. I tend to do less listening and to jump to the planning stage sooner than I would otherwise.)

Always have the conference in the teacher's classroom, unless there is a good reason not to. By meeting in the teacher's classroom, you convey a message that *you* are there to help *him or her*. In addition, you have at your disposal the materials the teacher is using and samples of the students' work, should those be needed during the conversation.

Facilitating Individual Conferences

Starting Out. Begin the conference by briefly reviewing what happened at the last conference. Summarize the topics you and the teacher discussed the last time you met and the next steps that you and the teacher had planned to take. Indicate to the teacher that you want to address the next steps but that first you want to know how things are going for him or her. Here's what this part of the conversation might sound like:

> I have my notes from our last conference here. Let's see, we discussed your use of conferences to get to know the students at the beginning of the year. We looked at the notes you had from a couple of running records, and you shared that the information from your conferences with students had been really valuable. We talked about one student, Maggie, who had been puzzling you, and I offered to read with her and give you feedback before you decided whether to refer her to the Building Support Team. You set a goal of implementing your reading centers, and we agreed to talk about them at this meeting. This may still be your concern, but something else may have happened in the meantime. So, I want to begin by asking, How are things going?

When a literacy coach starts an individual conference in this manner, he or she accomplishes several things. First, the literacy coach provides a helpful review of what was discussed at the last conference. Second, the literacy coach focuses attention on the work at hand. Without such a focus, conferences often meander, resulting in chitchat, complaining, or rambling that often lacks a purpose.

Listening. When a literacy coach asks how things are going—after reviewing the past meeting and the goals for the current meeting—the literacy coach transfers some control of the conference to the teacher. Even when conferences are held weekly, a lot can happen between meetings. The literacy coach's inquiry gives the teacher an opportunity to share whatever is on her mind, and it gives the literacy coach an opportunity to listen and learn about the teacher's concerns. In this way, the literacy coach shifts from being the initiator of the conference to being a listener. Listening is at the heart of effective literacy coaching.

Steering. The literacy coach needs to facilitate the conference in a manner that keeps it focused yet allows the teacher to provide direction as well. If a new topic has arisen since the last meeting, the literacy coach may want to ask a question such as, "Last time we agreed to talk about narrative writing. Today I hear that you are concerned about revision. Which would you like to focus on today?" If the teacher chooses the new topic, then the literacy coach may want to ask the teacher if it would be agreeable to put the previously agreed upon topic on the list of items to discuss the next time they meet.

Throughout the conference, the literacy coach should monitor the conversation for focus. In any conversation, the individuals involved will digress, and that's fine as long as they return to the topic at hand. In fact, a conference that is overly focused may feel too intense for the participants. The literacy coach and teacher will want to feel free to interject humor, examples, spur-of-the-moment ideas, and other interruptions into the conversation. However, then they will want to return to the topic. If as a literacy coach you find yourself working with someone who easily gets off the topic, you will want to have some tactics for steering the conversation back. You might make any of the following statements:

- "That's a great new topic for discussion. I'm going to jot that down on my note sheet under 'Topics for Future Discussion.'"
- "I love thinking divergently, and it looks like you do, too. If we're not careful, we'll never get back to the original topic!"
- "I love sharing teaching stories with you. Should we have lunch next week to tell some more?"
- "I need your help in getting back to the topic. If we don't, I'll run out of time before my next appointment."

Note that in each of these examples, the statement focuses on "I" or perhaps "we." In other words, the literacy coach states his or her needs or concerns, rather than making observations or judgments about the teacher's needs or concerns.

Planning. Every conference should serve as a springboard to action. State the goal that the teacher is working on and make sure that you and the teacher have the same understanding of it. Then think of next steps. It often is useful to brainstorm a variety of possible steps and then decide which to pursue. You and the teacher always should have at least one action step that will lead toward that goal, and that step should be taken before the next conference.

Possible actions steps are listed in Table 5. As this list implies, developing action steps can take a literacy coach and teacher in a variety of

Table 5
Possible Action Steps

● ● ●

Teacher	Literacy Coach
Try a new instructional practice.	Locate teaching materials.
Use a new assessment technique.	Provide professional articles.
Refine an existing practice.	Read professional literature.
Observe one student closely.	Demonstrate instructional practices.
Alter student conferencing practices.	Observe one child closely.
Organize instructional time differently.	Locate a classroom to visit.
Observe another teacher.	Participate in a conference with a parent.
Observe the coach modeling a practice.	Meet with the principal.
Reorganize the classroom.	Conduct research at the library.
Read an article.	Locate children's literature.
Attend a workshop.	Seek and evaluate assessment tools.
Plan with other teachers.	Attend a workshop.
Meet with the principal for advice, resources, or both.	Confer with other coaches.
Confer with a parent.	Summarize research findings.
View a videotape.	
Write reflections.	
Find new materials.	
Conduct research at the library.	

directions. The most effective literacy coaches are able to think creatively with the teacher to explore all options. This process may stimulate some literacy coaches who are naturally divergent thinkers, but it may produce stress for literacy coaches who don't easily generate multiple ideas. If you fall into the latter group, you may want to copy Table 5 (with your own additions and modifications) and tape it to your clipboard. Then you and each teacher can refer to it as you seek action steps. Another approach, if you and a teacher really feel stuck, is to end the conference early and then meet the next day to finish the conference. (A word of caution: Don't let more than one day pass between the initial and latter parts of the conference or you'll lose momentum.)

Scheduling. Don't end an individual conference without scheduling the next one. Always carry your calendar with you and, when you remind the teacher of the next conference (via an e-mail message or a note in his or her mailbox), request that he or she bring a calendar as well.

Recording and Distributing. Take notes on the entire conference. After the conference, make a copy of the notes for the teacher as well as the principal. Maintain the original notes in a file folder that you keep for that particular teacher and that you carry to every conference with him or her.

I find it helpful to use a form on which to take notes. The form guides my facilitation of the meeting by reminding me of each step of the conference, and it provides an easy format for recording notes. On the next page you will find a blank copy of my note-taking form, and Figure 1 provides a sample of how the form might be completed. My wish is that each literacy coach will adapt the form to make it the most useful for his or her own work.

Conclusion

Individual conferences are an important part of a literacy coach's duties. These conferences enable both the literacy coach and the teacher to focus on needs, strengths, and concerns unique to that teacher or of highest priority to him or her. Successful individual conferences depend on the literacy coach's facilitation. Among the facilitation skills useful for individual conferences are

- preparing for the conference by reviewing previous notes and thinking ahead to what may be discussed at the upcoming conference;
- taking careful notes to track action steps, the next meeting time and date, and current and future goals;

Individual Conference Record Sheet

• • •

Teacher _____   Grade _____

Coach _____   Date _____

How It's Going:

Items Discussed:

For Future Discussion:

Next Steps

Goal:

Action Steps:

     Teacher:

     Coach:

Next Meeting:

Bring to Next Meeting:

Distribute:
___ coach
___ teacher
___ principal

Figure 1
Sample Individual Conference Record Sheet

• • •

Teacher ___Ann Smith_____ Grade _3_____

Coach _____Brenda Fuller_____ Date _10/14/03___

How It's Going:
Ann is implementing reading workshop for the first time. She did a lot of conferencing in September, which she found very helpful. Now she is trying to implement guided reading groups. However, she is having a hard time focusing on the guided reading group in front of her because the other students are interrupting her and/or are not doing what they're supposed to be doing in their centers.

Items Discussed:
Reasons for kids' interruptions: They don't know what to do at centers; they are arguing with each other; they are used to her help during center time.

Options other than centers: Discussed having the kids read, record, and journal during workshop time.

Reviewed Ann's goals for the kids who are not with her in guided reading: She wants them learning but she also wants them in one place and quiet so she can focus on GR.

For Future Discussion:
Frequency of conferences, additional assessments to use

Next Steps
Goal: Develop alternative to centers during workshop time.

Action Steps:
> Teacher: Temporarily reduce centers to a listening station, a reading station, and a writing station until she develops a plan for workshop time.

> Coach: Provide Ann with description of how Sharon Taberski sets up her workshop time. Ask principal if Ann and Brenda can visit Washington School to observe their reading workshop.

Next Meeting: October 21, 2003

Bring to Next Meeting: Ideas for Ann's workshop, calendar to schedule visit to Washington School

Distribute:
___ coach
___ teacher
___ principal

● keeping the conversation comfortable but focused; and

● following through on commitments in a reliable manner.

As discussed in chapter 4, there are certain qualities and skills that are essential for all literacy coaching. This chapter has provided tools to maximize the literacy coach's effectiveness in working with individuals. The next chapter builds the literacy coach's toolkit further by providing practical methods for working with teams and study groups.

ADDITIONAL RESOURCES FOR LITERACY COACHES

Fournies, F.F. (2000). *Coaching for improved work performance* (Rev. ed.). New York: McGraw-Hill.

Lyons, C.A. (2002). Becoming an effective literacy coach: What does it take? In E.M. Rodgers & G.S. Pinnell (Eds.), *Learning from teaching in literacy education: New perspectives on professional development* (pp. 93–118). Portsmouth, NH: Heinemann.

Lyons, C.A., & Pinnell, G.S. (2001). *Systems for change in literacy education: A guide to professional development*. Portsmouth, NH: Heinemann.

CHAPTER 7

How Do I Coach Teacher Teams and Study Groups?

- Why should I coach teacher teams and study groups?

- Are all teams and groups the same?

- What should I do when one person dominates a team or group?

- What should I do about people who speak too much or too little?

- How do I prevent a team or group meeting from being a gripe session?

- What should I do when team or group members disagree or debate?

- How do I facilitate a study group?

- How do I facilitate an inquiry group?

L iteracy coaches divide their time among many duties. Conferring with individual teachers is a part of their work, but so is meeting with teams of teachers and study groups. This chapter looks at these coaching duties that require the ability to work with small groups of teachers. First, we'll look at team meetings in general—their purpose and how to make them effective—and then we'll discuss two unique kinds of teams: study groups and inquiry groups.

Why Have Team Meetings?

Team meetings make sense for several reasons. Overall, they encourage collaboration and help literacy coaches make good use of time by meeting with several teachers at once. More specifically, different kinds of team meetings serve different purposes, as outlined in Table 6.

Table 6
Team Meetings and Their Purposes

• • •

Team Type	Team Description	Team Purposes
Grade-level	Includes all teachers who teach at a particular grade level	• Supports teachers in a team format in which they often work anyway • Provides for easy sharing of instructional materials • Focuses all members of the group on the same standards and curricula • Addresses developmental needs of students at that grade
Unit	Includes a group of teachers who work together to serve the same group of students or teach the same discipline; for example, all teachers who work with a category of special education students or all teachers who teach social studies	• Supports teachers in a team format in which they often work anyway • Addresses unique needs of students in special programs • Focuses all members of the group on the same disciplinary knowledge, practices, or standards
Interest or need	Includes teachers who have the same interest in a particular instructional approach, literacy topic, or teaching struggle; for example, teachers who are implementing guided reading, teachers interested in using literature to teach social studies, or teachers struggling to meet the needs of English-language learners Inquiry groups and study groups are two special kinds of interest or need teams.	• Brings together teachers with shared interests who might not otherwise find each other • Supports focused exploration of a topic • Addresses pressing issues • Creates conversation across grade levels and units • Creates a pilot team to implement a new program or approach on a trial basis

As you can see by looking at the table, team meetings can accomplish a lot. They bring together teachers with shared interests, teaching assignments, or problems. They enable groups of educators to look at a topic in a focused way. They develop support systems for educators who might not otherwise work together. And they provide for the sharing of resources and knowledge specific to a group of teachers.

Facilitating Team Meetings

Some aspects of the facilitation of team meetings are the same as the facilitation of individual conferences. In both cases, the literacy coach should get the conversation started, check how things have been going for the teachers since the last meeting, assist teachers in focusing on the topic at hand, plan the next steps—including setting a goal and deciding who will do what—schedule the next meeting, take notes, and duplicate and distribute the notes. Chapter 5 gives more detailed suggestions for performing each of these duties.

However, there are some unique aspects to facilitating a meeting with a team of teachers, rather than an individual teacher. Most of these aspects involve the challenge of bringing individuals together to work as a team. There are the assumptions in western society that groups of people automatically know how to communicate and that understanding will automatically occur if communication takes place. People may realize that it helps to review the rules of working as a group and that a facilitator can bring the group back if they get off track, but basically, the assumption is that people know how to work together and communicate in a group.

My thinking on this matter has been influenced by the work of Elizabeth Ellsworth. In her book, *Teaching Positions: Difference, Pedagogy, and the Power of Address* (1997), Ellsworth writes about the difficulty of communicative dialogue. In fact, she concludes that full understanding among individuals is impossible—that communicative dialogue is to an extent wishful thinking—but that we need to continue to communicate nonetheless. In the process of failing to communicate what we intended, we still communicate something, and we have no choice but to keep trying. I'm oversimplifying Ellsworth's book: It presents ideas about teaching and about understanding that I've found in no other book on education. Although Ellsworth's thinking is complex and unfamiliar to many educators, I'd encourage experienced literacy coaches to take a look at her book, because it will enhance literacy coaches' understanding of the challenges and possibilities of the conversations in which they are engaging.

So, it's difficult for groups to collaborate successfully. However, literacy coaches still need to be able to facilitate such group work. The following are suggestions for doing so.

Honor varying levels of participation. Group leaders often are outgoing people and, therefore, tend to assume that everyone else in the group should be that way, too. Of course, some people are more outgoing than others, so for some people active group participation means sitting quietly while their minds race with the ideas they are hearing. The good thing about facilitating a group of adults is that most participants know how they best participate in a group. Therefore, I'd encourage literacy coaches to ask group members to talk about their participation preferences when the group first meets, and then to check in with the group members periodically to see if everyone is feeling comfortable with their own—and others'—level of participation.

For a literacy coach facilitating a group meeting, the greatest difficulty relating to members' participation is usually the individuals who talk too much or not at all. Often, the process of checking in with group members about their participation levels helps to even out individual members' levels of participation, but if it doesn't, the literacy coach may want to talk to the quiet or talkative participants individually, outside the group setting. In doing so, the literacy coach's goals should be to check if the individual is comfortable with his or her level of participation and to see if he or she thinks the rest of the group is comfortable with it. If the literacy coach goes beyond this point to telling the talkative person that he or she needs to quiet down or the quiet person that he or she needs to speak up, the literacy coach may end up in the uncomfortable position of being held responsible for the group's functioning and being resented by those individuals he or she has singled out.

Addressing disagreement. People don't all see things the same way; sometimes they disagree. Yet in a team meeting, disagreement often creates distress. Despite the reality that all people experience disagreement from time to time, we somehow become uncomfortable or even embarrassed when disagreement occurs. I don't know what is at the root of this phenomenon, but I do suspect that it occurs more often among women than men. Females raised in a traditional manner in our society are raised to be agreeable so it is even more difficult for such women than for others to voice disagreement or to hear others disagreeing (Tannen, 1994). Although many females are no longer raised in this manner, many societal structures still convey similar messages, and many women subconsciously conform to these messages.

Regardless of whether one is male or female, raised with traditional norms or not, disagreement occurs and causes a bit of a struggle for those participating in group conversations. Literacy coaches can assist groups in dealing with disagreement. First, as a literacy coach, you should demonstrate comfort with disagreement. Show acceptance and curiosity when others disagree with you, and disagree with others in a manner that is without judgment—merely a disagreement, not anything to cause shame, and always done respectfully. You may recall that in chapter 5, I defined true respect as that which is not about imposing one's own goals on another. The same is true about respect in disagreement. The goal is to have a voice in the conversation but not in a way that leaves others feeling like they can't do the same. James Flaherty (1999) suggests that the coach's goal is "mutual freedom of expression" (p. 56) among all participants.

In addition, ask group members what they want to do about disagreements. They'll probably look at you in amazement because this kind of conversation usually doesn't take place in groups, and they'll probably quickly assure you that disagreement is fine. When a disagreement does occur, however, you may want to ask again. Then group members may better understand why you asked that question.

Addressing competing claims. One source of disagreement—or at least one source of support for one's disagreement—is competing claims. For example, one group member says that a teaching practice will work well with students, and another group member states, "Not with *my* students." Or one member of the group makes a claim about what works and another says, "The research says the opposite." How does a literacy coach help in such situations?

First, model calm acceptance of disagreement, again. You might even chuckle and observe, "This happens a lot in education, doesn't it? We face competing claims and have to decide how to resolve them—or if they can be resolved at all." In this manner, you are making disagreement visible and acceptable.

At this point, you may be wondering if my suggestions are a bit naïve. After all, people in groups often make competing claims to seem superior, to avoid admitting they are wrong, or to obtain some power. Shouldn't a literacy coach try to stop this behavior? I'd suggest that you don't. First of all, as a literacy coach you might guess why individuals are making competing claims, but you don't know for certain. Second, if you try to overrule these individuals based on your assumption that they have questionable motives, you merely perpetuate the power struggle and the attempt to prove another person wrong. It would be wiser to respond to what the individuals have said, not what they may be thinking.

If members of a group make competing claims about "the research," it's easy to ask them to share the research. Those who are merely posturing will usually "forget" or become too busy to locate the research they've mentioned. Those who are serious will share the research, which can lead to a valuable discussion about how educators can make decisions when research studies produce competing results. A word of caution: If you ask someone to produce supporting research, do so in a neutral manner. Don't say, "Can you prove it by showing us the research?" or something similar that sounds like a challenge. Rather, say something such as,

> I hear that we have competing claims being made about the research. If you'd give me some citations, I'll track down the research you are referring to. I'll also see if there is anything in the professional literature that would help us understand these competing claims.

If group members make competing claims about their students and what works in their own classrooms, you may want to suggest the following criteria for determining an effective practice:

- It improves students' work and attitudes.
- It is consistent with what you believe about learning, literacy, and teaching.
- It fits the parameters in which you must work, including standards and curricula.

None of these issues—effectiveness of practice, competing research claims, resolving differences, and struggling for power in groups—is easy to resolve, and most issues will not be resolved during the duration of a team's collaboration. That in itself is an important concept for literacy coaches to remember and to help group members consider. Look back at the list of purposes that small groups serve. Nowhere does it say that small groups will resolve all differences or determine the best practices. Small groups provide support, focus, attention, and opportunities for collaboration.

Addressing intimidation. Literacy coaches occasionally find themselves working with dysfunctional groups in which one member intimidates the others. This unhealthiness manifests itself in various ways. For example, group members may always agree publicly, even while disagreeing privately; the domineering group member may control the conversation by providing cues regarding what the others should say or believe; or disagreement on the part of any member may be treated with panic, rudeness, or by ostracizing him or her. Such situations happen temporarily in groups, when addressing particular topics or when the group is just not at its best, but a truly unhealthy group has this problem consistently, and it is usually the result of one member.

This is among the most difficult group problems to address. Literacy coaches need to think carefully about these situations and might benefit from talking with trusted colleagues to get additional perspectives. Among the options available to literacy coaches are to ask the intimidating staff member to change his or her behavior or leave the group, or to encourage group members to change their manner of participating. However, each of these tactics is likely to backfire. Any dysfunctional group, whether it's a family or a work group, does not correct itself easily. In fact, systems theorists tell us that such a group functions like any other system. Its primary function is to preserve itself, and it does so despite efforts to intervene.

This is a discouraging picture. It frustrates me to have few successful tactics for literacy coaches in this situation. However, I do offer some advice. First, don't dismiss every group that struggles. The situation described in this section occurs only occasionally. Use all your best coaching skills with a group that is not going easily, and label it dysfunctional with caution. Get advice from a colleague before you give up.

Second, if there truly is an intimidator among the teachers, have a conversation with the principal. This is a supervisory matter, and it should not be up to a literacy coach to address it. In cases where a staff member has gained the ability to exert so much power, he or she frequently has succeeded in intimidating the principal, too. Nonetheless, this is a matter for the school administrator to address. It is not a literacy coaching matter.

Third, in such instances, the literacy coach may need to limit the large-group meetings he or she leads. Perhaps the literacy coach can have two-person meetings instead to support collaboration but to avoid the necessity of including the intimidating staff member.

Finally, on occasion, a brave and patient literacy coach can ask the intimidating staff member for assistance, such as conducting a research review or providing an overview of what occurs in his or her classroom. This approach enables that staff member to feel valued and recognized. As you might guess, this approach can backfire by giving the intimidating staff member too much attention, but it might be worth a try.

The problem of an intimidating group member occurs only occasionally, but when it does, it can become the focal point of a group's functioning. Moreover, this problem can cause a literacy coach to feel overwhelmed and inept. I advise literacy coaches in these situations to dig deep into their coaching toolkits and make best use of every skill they have. In addition, I advise literacy coaches to stay calm and to avoid taking anything that happens personally. Finally, I encourage literacy coaches to remember that the intimidating group member is still a human being, not a monster, and to approach that person in a humane and reasonable manner.

The Content of Team Meetings

So, what are team meetings *about*? Whereas individual conferences start with the individual teacher's interests and concerns, team members often come together with a variety of interests and concerns. Where should the team start? How does a literacy coach facilitate the process? Some literacy coaches determine ahead of time the topic that will be discussed or prepare a sort of miniworkshop for the team meeting. This isn't what I'd recommend. Let me illustrate this point with an example about a real-life coaching experience.

I recall the first time I began coaching two literacy coaches at an elementary school. They arranged a schedule of grade-level team meetings on a day when I'd be visiting, then they asked me what I needed in order to prepare. I now know they were shocked when I replied, "Nothing. We'll just see what the teams bring to the table." These literacy coaches were surprised that I'd approach group meetings without an agenda. However, I believed that if I began with an agenda, I would establish a relationship that wasn't a coaching relationship. I would appear to know what the teachers needed and to be the expert who would provide that.

When the teachers came into the meeting, I said something such as,

> The purpose of these meetings is to support you in developing the kinds of classrooms you want, teaching in ways you know are effective, and guiding your students to be successful readers and writers. The agenda will be set by your needs and interests as well as the challenges presented by your students. I'm not here as the expert but as one of several experts in this room. We all are experts about some things and can share our expertise with each other. So, let's start with this question: How's it going?

The coaches I was coaching in that setting later revealed that they had felt panicked by my introduction. They were sure that the meeting would be a waste of time because the teachers would share ineffective practices, or no practices at all, and would raise issues that weren't important. To a degree, the other coaches were right. When there is no agenda, the conversation sometimes has false starts and the topics initially raised may not be the most important ones. However, at the beginning of a coach–team relationship, the *process* is more important than the *content*. Your objective as literacy coach should be to establish roles, relationships, and processes for communicating with one another and working together. The content will increasingly be the focus as the group continues to meet.

As a team starts working together, you as a literacy coach will indeed hear things that you disagree with as teachers share their goals and even some of their teaching practices. I'd encourage you to tolerate almost anything that's said. If you don't, you will convey to the group members that the meeting isn't really about their concerns and that they all aren't respected by you as knowing some things as experts. Instead, the teachers will feel manipulated. When you disrupt the flow of conversation to steer it away from teachers' ideas, you imply that you are only pretending that you are all equals and that you all have expertise—because that will make the team feel good and you appear nice—but you really have the power and control, and you'll use it to make sure that they stick to ideas you agree with. Clearly, that's not the message you want to convey, particularly at your first meeting with the group.

You should not think, however, that I'm totally without standards for discussions during team meetings. There is one set of statements that I'll dispute or disrupt even at the earliest team meetings—statements that are put-downs of the students. If a team member uses negative labels for students—for example, calling them all lazy—or makes racist or classist statements about students, such as "The kids from the projects [a low-income housing development] would never be able to pass that test," I do challenge those statements. They violate deeply held values that I need to honor to maintain my personal moral integrity. Note that I'm not speaking about values I hold about teaching or literacy but rather values essential to my spiritual and moral self. You need to be true to yourself, too, and identify those core values that you cannot let anyone violate.

Listening. Make clear that you are listening to what the team members share. Take notes. Check to see if you've recorded teachers' concerns accurately by asking follow-up questions to clarify. And restate what each teacher says in an active listening manner. You want to be sure that you have indeed heard team members accurately, and you want to ensure that the team knows you take their ideas seriously. Use wait time. After it appears that the last person has spoken, then ask, "What else?" Often, the most serious concerns are raised near the end of the sharing time.

Focusing. After an initial round of sharing progress and concerns, the team members probably will need some help in moving ahead. A good strategy for literacy coaches is to read their notes aloud to remind the group of both the successes and challenges that have been shared. Then, ask the group members to think about prioritizing the concerns that were shared. Remind the team members that they will be together for a while, having regular meetings with you, so there will be time to address many of the concerns that were shared but that there is a need to start someplace. Then lead the discussion to determine priority topics with which to begin.

Taking action. A team can easily carry on for several meetings and several months without really doing anything. Teachers can become accustomed to team meetings as opportunities to share their opinions and ideas and to commiserate about problems. These aren't bad reasons for coming together, and they may be what helps the team to continue, especially at the start. However, these are not adequate reasons for teams to meet. One of your goals as a literacy coach will be to move the team to action, to doing something differently. Here are some strategies for moving the group to action:

- After reviewing concerns and prioritizing one to address first, ask the group members to brainstorm what might be contributing to the problem. List these factors on the left side of a T-chart (a chart with two columns and space for a heading at the top of each column). Then ask the group members to brainstorm possible ways to address each factor, and list those responses in the right-hand column. After completing the brainstorming, highlight the most significant factors and the most realistic approaches to addressing those factors.

- Ask, "If a genie landed on your desk and granted you anything to solve this problem, what would you request?" (Don't allow the answer, "Make it go away.") Encourage team members to shout out their answers quickly while you jot them down. Then talk about the possible solutions, prioritize them, and create steps for implementing one or more.

- If the topic seems perplexing to team members, offer to provide one article on the topic at the next meeting. Use the team time to read and discuss the article and the solutions it proposes. Then plan which of those solutions the team would like to try.

- When dealing with a recurring problem, give each team member a pad of sticky notes and ask all of them to quickly write their ideas for solving the problem, one per sticky note. Draw large circles on chart paper or a blackboard and label them "Tried—won't work," "Tried—could work," "Would like to try," "Would like to try but don't have resources," "Don't think this will work," and "Not sure." Ask each individual to place his or her notes in the appropriate circles, then discuss the items as a group. If you want to go a step further, ask team members to review the notes and, in silence before any discussion takes place, move them to different circles as they see fit.

When the team has generated possible solutions to a problem and selected some to try, create an action plan. Include in that plan statements of what will be done and by whom, and set reasonable deadlines. Setting deadlines will be an interesting task. In education, we have a tendency to give ourselves long deadlines, longer than in many other workplaces. This probably is due to the complexity of our field and the number of unexpected tasks that arise on a regular basis. Nonetheless, the longer we give ourselves to do something, the more likely we are to postpone doing it. Try to set realistic deadlines but push yourselves to take the action steps as soon as possible.

Problem solving. When it comes to problems, human beings are sort of funny. I say this in the gentlest and most respectful manner, but, really, we are rather odd. We spend a fair amount of time puzzling over problems and pestering our work colleagues and family members about them. It certainly appears that we want a solution to our problems, but we can become so attached to the problems and so comfortable with the expenditure of energy on them, that in some ways we don't want to give them up. Think about all the energy you put into complaining about your spouse, feeling ashamed of your weight, or worrying about your children. What would you *do* with yourself if these problems were solved? I'm joking to a certain extent, but not entirely. It's pretty easy to become attached to our problems, which certainly can be true of teams as well as individuals.

A key step in problem solving with teams is asking the team members what their situation will look like and sound like when the problem is solved. (You can use this strategy with individuals, too, but it seems that individuals can more easily move on. The synergy of a group can perpetuate a problem or the quest for a solution.) Identifying what the situation will look like when the problem is solved creates a vision of life without the problem and helps the group members recognize when it is time to move on to new issues. A literacy coach can facilitate this process by helping the team members establish benchmarks for how they will gauge their success. After those benchmarks are established, it is essential to determine how they will be measured. Here is an example of how one literacy coach helped a team establish benchmarks and determine how to measure them:

●●●●●

Marion, a literacy coach working with an interdisciplinary primary team, helped the team set a goal of increasing student motivation to read. Then she guided the team in developing a plan to monitor whether they were meeting that goal. The first step was to think about signs that the goal had been met, so Marion asked, "If you reach the goal of increasing student motivation to read, what will you see and hear that tells you the goal was met?" The team began making a three-column chart. In the first column they listed what their classrooms and their students would look like and sound like if the students were motivated to read. Items in this column included "Students read at home when reading is not assigned," and "Students voluntarily discuss what they are reading."

Then Marion asked, "What tools could you use to determine if your classrooms and your students really did look and sound this way?" The team then looked at each item in the first column and identified a tool that could help them assess that item in the second column. Items in this column included a parent survey and teacher observation notes taken during shared reading. Marion asked a third question, "If you use these tools to look for the signs that the goal was met, how will you know that the goal was met?" In other words, Marion was asking the group members to determine criteria for goal achievement. The group completed the third column of the chart with these indicators, including, "There will be a 50% increase in parent reporting that students are reading at home," and "Analysis of teacher observation notes indicates a depth and interest in reading on the part of the students."

After this brainstorming process, Marion asked, "Which of the signs that students are motivated, listed in the first column, seem most useful in showing that the goal has been met?" The team discussed the list of indicators of meeting their goal and listed them from most useful to least useful. Marion asked, "Are there any items toward the bottom of this list that are of such limited usefulness that they should be eliminated?" The team pared the list by two items. Finally, Marion asked, "Can we develop a plan for collecting the data and looking at the indicators related to each of the items in the first column?" The team developed a list of the kinds of data to be collected and discussed how each of them could collect some of it. (See Table 7 for their completed chart.)

Another step in problem solving is to monitor progress and adjust practices as the team members implement them. This will be important work for the team throughout the length of its work. In other words, it would not be good to establish a goal and a plan to collect data to see if the goal is being reached, and then to do nothing about it until the end of the

Table 7
One Team's Plan for Monitoring Success

• • •

Looks and/or Sounds Like	Tool for Collecting Data	Indicator That Goal Has Been Met
Students read when they have free time at school	Observation of students' use of free time conducted by teaching assistant four times per year	50% increase of reading during free time between first and fourth observations
Students read at home when reading is not assigned	Parent survey completed at fall and spring parent–teacher conferences	50% increase in parent reporting of student reading at home
Students indicate that reading is a favorite activity	Student reading interest inventory	Pre- and postmeasures indicating 50% increase in positive responses
Students voluntarily discuss what they are reading	Teacher notes taken during shared reading; literacy coach observation notes taken during literature circles; anecdotal data collected from principal, lunchroom supervisors, and playground supervisors	Analysis of notes demonstrating depth and interest on the part of students

implementation period. Instead, as team members implement new practices, they need to gauge their progress along the way and make alterations in their practices as they go. Here's an illustration from the group Marion was working with in the previous example:

• • • • •

Midway through the year, it became evident to the teachers that students were indeed voluntarily discussing what they read, but the children were doing so to please the teachers, not because they were truly interested in the reading. As the team members considered this matter, they realized that some of the children were reading books for early readers that were so simple that they had little content. There was no "story" for the students to comprehend and appreciate. So the teachers adjusted their sources of data to include the discussion of materials that the teachers used during read-aloud time. In addition, the teachers added an action step for themselves, which was to find more meaningful books that early readers could enjoy.

This approach to problem solving truly is teacher action research. It engages teachers in posing solutions to problems and then monitoring their success in implementing the solutions and reaching their goals. A team can be a wonderful support system for such efforts, and a literacy coach is essential in guiding the team through the process.

Recording and distributing. Be sure to keep notes of what the group talks about and the action plan that is developed. A reproducible record sheet for team meetings can be found on the next page; Figure 2 shows a sample of a completed record sheet. This sheet is quite similar to the record sheet for individual conferences, but it has space for more details of the action plan, which is important because more individuals are involved. After the meeting, make copies of the record sheet and give them to all team members as well as your principal.

Study Groups

Teams often examine the work of others when looking for solutions to problems. For example, it is common to turn to professional literature for ideas, in addition to visiting colleagues' classrooms and attending workshops and courses. No team has all the answers, and it is valuable to look outside the team for additional ideas. However, some teams are formed with the primary intent of looking outside themselves for ideas. These teams, referred to as study groups, most often form for the purpose of reading a book or series of articles on a topic of shared interest. Literacy coaches need many of the same facilitation skills with study groups as with other teams, but they need to attend to some special issues as well.

Time. One of the first struggles identified by many study groups is a lack of time for reading. This is a problem the entire education profession faces. It is essential that educators remain familiar with the literature in the field, just as it is in any other profession. However, teachers have no time in the school day for professional reading, and their evenings often are used for other work-related duties. (Not to mention that teachers have families and friends and would like to enjoy time with them.) So, where does a study group find time to read a book?

There are a number of approaches to this dilemma. The ideal solution is to create time, say, by giving each participant a one-day substitute teacher

Team Meeting Record Sheet

• • •

Group Members _____

Coach _____ Date _____

Grade Level/Unit/Focus of Group _____

How It's Going:

Topics Discussed:

For Future Discussion:

Next Steps

Goal:

Action Steps:

Who	Task	Completion Date

Next Meeting:

Bring to Next Meeting:

Distribute:
___ team members
___ principal
___ coach

Figure 2
Sample Team Meeting Record Sheet

• • •

Group Members _____Monica, Bill, Leslie, Consuela_____

Coach _____Delia_____ Date _____3/22/04_____

Grade Level/Unit/Focus of Group _____Grade 6, LD Resource_____

How It's Going:
All four teachers have been conducting writing conferences with their students. The kids have been doing projects in social studies and are now writing up their findings to share with their classmates and the kids in the other sixth-grade classrooms. Keeping the other kids on task during the conferences is the biggest problem right now.

Topics Discussed:
● What has been tried to keep kids on task: Minilesson on expectations; point system; check with buddy if you don't know what to do
● What else might be tried: More minilessons; ticket for one teacher interruption per week, but no more, for neediest students; Monica to provide more assistance to all kids, not just LD kids; use teacher aides or parent volunteers; make buddy editing more focused

For Future Discussion:
Grammar and when to correct it in writing

Next Steps

Goal: Try a new way to keep kids on task during writing workshop
Action Steps:

Who	Task	Completion Date
Delia	Share Nancie Atwell's ideas for keeping kids on task. Put a copy in teachers' mailboxes.	3/29/04
Monica	Circulate throughout the classroom while the classroom teacher holds conferences.	4/5/04
Bill	Ask a parent volunteer to help during writing workshop time.	3/29/04
Leslie and Consuela	Revise the buddy editing sheet to make it easier to use.	3/29/04

Next Meeting: 3/29/04
Bring to Next Meeting: Atwell resource from Delia

Distribute:
___ team members
___ principal
___ coach

in exchange for participation in the study group. (The participant may need more than a day to read a book, but supplying a substitute teacher for him or her provides at least some additional reading time.) However, in an era of tight budgets, this approach is not possible in most school settings. Another approach is to create a reward for study group participation. In states where teachers need to earn graduate credit or credit-equivalent units (CEUs) in order to renew their teaching licenses, it may be possible to provide CEUs for a study group's members; in this way, each teacher gains the time that he or she otherwise would have spent getting CEUs in another manner. Other rewards might be $50 for classroom materials to implement the ideas in the book, or funding to attend a conference on a related issue. (You might ask your parent–teacher association for help with this funding.) Such rewards don't actually provide additional time, but they do make the expenditure of time easier for teachers to bear.

Beyond creating time and rewards for teachers, a literacy coach might find expedient ways for the study group members to read the book. One option is for a parent volunteer to make a recording of the book on audiotape or CD and provide it to busy teachers, who can listen to it while they drive to and from work, jog, run errands, and so on. Another option is for the group members to divide the book's chapters among themselves, with each group member being responsible for reading one or two chapters and summarizing them for the other group members. A third option is for the group to select only certain chapters that they all will read, leaving the remaining chapters as optional reading.

Here's an idea I learned from Jamie Myers, a faculty member at Pennsylvania State University, where I attended graduate school. I once asked Jamie how he managed to keep up with his reading, and he shared this tip: Read the first chapter of a book, then read the last chapter, the second-last chapter, and so on, working your way back toward the first chapter. When the book starts to repeat itself, stop reading. If your study group is starved for time, this strategy might be worth an effort.

A final tip: When the time issue arises, literacy coaches might want to discuss with the group members their level of commitment and the number of hours they wish to spend on the given topic. For instance, a literacy coach might say, "This book provides strategies for helping students improve their writing. How many hours are you willing to commit to that topic?" Let's say the teachers agree that they'd be willing to spend 10 hours on the topic. The group might then realize that they need 90 minutes to discuss the book after they've read it (in two 45-minute sessions) and 90 minutes to reconvene after they've tried some ideas from the book. This would leave six hours for reading the book. Knowing this time allotment, group members could plan how best to use those six hours.

"Real" discussion. When literacy coaches seek to facilitate discussions of books read by study groups, they have a challenge similar to that of teachers trying to get students to discuss what they've read. The challenge is to create meaningful discussions that prompt reflection and sharing and enrich participants' experiences of what they read. The desire is to avoid creating discussions merely for the sake of discussions, simple question-and-answer sessions, or painful gatherings of group members in which attempts to share what they liked about the book are interspersed with long spells of silence.

So, how does a literacy coach facilitate a discussion? Remember something that Kathy Short has written and spoken about (Short, Kaufman, Kaser, Kahn, & Crawford, 1999; personal communication, October 28, 1994). Book discussions, like all discussions, have a natural cycle. They usually begin with conversation, often not even on the topic, until group members settle in and feel ready to tackle the task at hand. Be patient with such conversation when it occurs in a study group. However, if the conversation doesn't eventually flow into a discussion of the book that was read, use your facilitation skills to move it along. The following strategies will help you do so.

- Use a strategy called "Save the Last Word for Me" (Short, Harste, & Burke, 1996). Ask each group member to select a pithy quotation from the book and share it with the others. After one person shares his or her chosen quotation, that person should remain silent until every other person in the group has had a chance to respond to the quotation. Then, the person who introduced the quotation has the last word by sharing why he or she selected that quotation and why it is significant to him or her. This strategy ensures that everyone in the group has a turn to speak and often serves as a good icebreaker.

- Before the discussion session, invite study group participants to mark the book with sticky notes as they read, noting passages that they'd like to discuss with the group.

- Ask each group member to write two "telegraph messages" about the book. One message would summarize its usefulness, and the other would summarize the group member's major question or concern about the book. Remind the group that telegraph messages need to be extremely brief because they are paid for by the word. Then ask group members to share their messages and discuss them.

- Invite each group member to write a reflection on the book for the first five minutes of the meeting. Then use the reflections as springboards for discussion.

- Ask group members to take turns providing a discussion-starter at each study group meeting. Talk a bit about what makes such an activity meaningful, and ask participants to draw on their experiences in creating meaningful discussions with their own students. (A side effect of this approach may be that teachers develop some discussion-starting strategies that they use with their own students as well.)

Differences and disagreements with the author. When a study group focuses its attention on someone else's writing, the group members are one step removed from their own work. Literacy coaches need to facilitate the process of connecting what group members read to what they are doing or might do. In addition, because the author of the book or journal article is not present and is likely a stranger to the group, it is much easier to criticize his or her work. It is also easier to make the author the "other." This means that, when the author raises unfamiliar or threatening ideas, readers dismiss the author as different from them, saying things such as, "She's a much different teacher than I am," or "He is in a much richer school than I am," or, the most common response, "That would never work with my students."

As with all literacy coaching duties, in these instances it is important to honor the group members' initial responses to what they have read. Then, as literacy coach you may want to use one or more of the following strategies to help group members make connections to what they've read.

- Make a Venn diagram highlighting differences and seeking similarities between the author and the study group members. Depending on the nature of the book, the diagram might focus on characteristics of the author's classroom and the group members' classrooms; qualities of the author as a teacher and of group members as teachers; or beliefs about teaching, learning, and literacy held by the author and by group members.

- Facilitate the group's development of a visual web of key ideas in the book, which can be drawn on a piece of chart paper. Then invite group members to use color-coded markers to indicate parts of the web that cohere with their own situations and parts that don't. First, discuss the parts of the web with which group members identify, then discuss the parts of the web that group members see as different from their situations.

- List the differences that group members see between their own situations and those presented in the book. Then, analyze each difference for its significance by distinguishing among those differences that matter and those that don't. Ask group members to focus on the differences that do matter but can be overcome. A reproducible chart that I've used for this activity can be found on the next page; Figure 3 offers a sample of the completed chart.

The success of a study group depends in large part on the quality of the conversation that its members have together. A skilled literacy coach will facilitate that conversation so that it is meaningful and authentic. In addition, the literacy coach will make the study group process as comfortable as possible by helping group members to find time to participate and to develop skills in questioning the author without necessarily dismissing the author altogether.

Inquiry Groups

Inquiry groups can be considered hybrids between general team meetings and study groups. Educators gather in inquiry groups when they want to explore a single topic or issue at great depth. The steps in the inquiry process are outlined in the section on coaching for inquiry in chapter 1. The skills used by coaches to steer an inquiry group will be the same skills outlined for the groups mentioned earlier in this chapter. In inquiry groups, however, literacy coaches will use two skills extensively: (1) gathering data and (2) making sense of data.

Gathering Data

Literacy coaches who facilitate inquiry groups need to think broadly about the meaning of the term *data* and help the group members to do so, too. Often, educators think that only numbers can serve as data, and frequently the only numbers considered are test scores. Although test scores could be part of the data considered by inquiry groups, there are many more kinds of data that will be useful. I'd encourage you to define data as any information that will help the inquiry group to learn more about the topic. Thus, data might include

- student observation notes;
- group members' reflections;
- samples of student work;
- parent surveys;
- running record notes;
- miscue analyses;
- checklists of observable student behaviors;

Comparing Our Group and the Author

• • •

Book:

Author:

Study Group Members:

Characteristic of Author	Different But the Difference Doesn't Matter	Different But the Difference Can Be Overcome	Different and the Difference Can't Be Overcome

Figure 3
Sample of Comparing Our Group and the Author

• • •

Book: *On Solid Ground: Strategies for Teaching Reading K–3*

Author: Sharon Taberski

Study Group Members: Bonnie, Ted, Paula, DeWayne, Marion

Characteristic of Author	Different But the Difference Doesn't Matter	Different But the Difference Can Be Overcome	Different and the Difference Can't Be Overcome
Works in urban school			X
Loops students in grades 2 and 3	X		
Has an extensive classroom library		X	
Works in a school with a schoolwide literacy focus		X	
Has class arranged without rows of desks		X	
Has a daily schedule that allows uninterrupted language arts time			X

- environmental scans, which assess classrooms and schools for their literacy-related content;
- information about school library use;
- information about technology access and use by students, parents, and teachers;
- interviews of students, parents, teachers, administrators, and community members; and
- research findings reported in professional literature.

This list is only a sampling of information that can be useful to an inquiry group. Literacy coaches probably will need to steer their inquiry groups toward thinking of other types of data that will be useful. Brainstorming a list and then prioritizing the data to be collected will be a helpful approach.

Making Sense of Data

Gathering all possible information from data is both a skill and an art. If an inquiry group wants to do a good job of data analysis, the group members may want to turn to one of the many books on practical teacher action research that provide tools for data analysis (see, for example, Hubbard & Power, 1993). If anyone from the staff has taken a course in research methods, he or she may be invited to help the group as well. However, common sense can lead group members to make a fair amount of sense from data. Here are some tips for data analysis:

Assign one member of the inquiry group to be the Tester of Assumptions. When the group draws a conclusion from the data, the Tester of Assumptions has the job of probing with two questions: (1) How do you know that? and (2) How confident are you that that is an accurate assumption? Group members won't always be certain that an assumption is accurate and support it unequivocally, and that is OK. (This is why we should avoid saying that research "proves" something; it only suggests or leads us to believe something is true. We rarely can be 100% sure.) By testing assumptions, however, we can avoid hunches that have little to support them.

Collect as many kinds of data as possible, and try to use one kind to support conclusions you are making about another kind. For instance, if a survey of parents indicates that their children never pay attention to spelling when writing at home, you might collect samples of nonacademic writing that their children have done to see if the samples support the parents' claims. Or if observation notes lead group members to believe that students are not motivated to read independently, you might collect student survey data to see if that hunch is supported.

Don't just list answers to open-ended survey questions. Rather, follow these steps: (a) Collect the answers in a typed list with triple spaces between each response; (b) cut the list apart, answer by answer; (c) take the resulting small strips of paper and sort them in ways that make sense. Do this sorting several times. It can lead to many insights. For example, an inquiry group examining reading in the content areas conducted a survey of middle school science and social studies teachers. When the survey responses were cut apart and sorted, the inquiry group members found that the responses could first be divided according to positive and negative responses. They sorted them this way and made note of which responses fell into which category. Then the inquiry group members found that the responses could be sorted another way, into groups according to whether they addressed teacher practices, beliefs, struggles, or questions. They sorted the responses this way and made note of which responses fell into which category. Finally, the inquiry group members found that the responses addressed a variety of topics in content area literacy, including vocabulary instruction, choice of instructional materials, student background knowledge, helping students to comprehend inferences, using graphs and pictures, and guiding students in deciding which information in text was most important. The inquiry group members sorted the responses this way and made notes of which responses fell into which category. Thus, when they were finished analyzing survey data, they had three sets of categories that helped them to understand the data from three different perspectives.

Make a chart of hypotheses that group members develop and the sources of data that support those hypotheses. Include a final column in the chart for data that challenge those hypotheses. This chart can serve as a record of the thinking of group members.

Don't be afraid to voice some hunches, even if you later find they are not supported by the data. As long as you don't jump to conclusions, it can be helpful to air possibilities.

Inquiry groups provide teachers with practices and support in exploring key issues of importance to them. However, the inquiry necessary for the success of such groups requires effective leadership. Literacy coaches can provide that leadership by providing general skills in group facilitation as well as specific skills in collecting data and making sense of those data. Many teachers approach data and data analysis with caution. They may feel unskilled in working with data and also may be skeptical that data can provide information that their own intuition cannot. Effective literacy coaches will help teachers to understand data and their use while honoring teachers' own craft knowledge. In addition, effective literacy coaches will guide teachers to identify practical data that will be useful in informing their instructional decisions, and they will guide teachers in analyzing those data in order to use them most effectively.

Conclusion

Coaching small groups demands many of the same skills as coaching individuals. However, when working with groups, literacy coaches need to attend to interpersonal dynamics among group members and the tendency for group members to subconsciously want to maintain their roles and statuses and perpetuate the functional style of the group. In addition, special groups, such as study groups and inquiry groups, require special literacy coaching skills.

The goal of small-group work, like the goal of individual work, is to assist participants in identifying and improving on their strengths as they find and solve problems. In addition, small-group work may have a goal of increasing collaboration among staff members. Such collaboration may be marred by individuals with whom the coach and others find difficulty working. This challenge has been touched upon in this chapter but it will be addressed at length in the next chapter.

ADDITIONAL RESOURCES FOR LITERACY COACHES

Achinstein, B. (2002). *Community, diversity, and conflict among schoolteachers: The ties that blind*. New York: Teachers College Press.

Anderson, G.L. (1998). Toward authentic participation: Deconstructing the discourses of participatory reforms in education. *American Educational Research Journal, 35*(4), 571–603.

Chandler, K., & Mapleton Teacher-Research Group. (1999). *Spelling inquiry: How one elementary school caught the mnemonic plague*. York, MN: Stenhouse.

Greenleaf, C., & Schoenbach, R. (2004). Building capacity for the responsive teaching of reading in the academic disciplines: Strategic inquiry designs for middle and high school teachers' professional development. In D.S. Strickland & M.L. Kamil (Eds.), *Improving reading achievement through professional development* (pp. 97–127). Norwood, MA: Christopher-Gordon.

Meyer, R.J., Larson, K., Zetterman, K., Ridder, K., & McKenzie, M. (1998). *Composing a teacher study group: Learning about inquiry in primary classrooms*. Mahwah, NJ: Erlbaum.

How Do I Coach in Difficult Situations?

CHAPTER 8

How Do I Deal With Difficult Teachers?

- What can I do to get teachers to open up to me?
- What should I do about teachers who don't want to change?
- How can I work with resistant teachers?

irst, I must confess that I dislike the title of this chapter: I don't like the word *deal* because it sounds as if teachers are objects with which literacy coaches must contend, not human beings and professional colleagues. And I don't like the word *difficult* because difficulty is in the eye of the beholder: What may look like a difficult person to you or me probably looks like a dedicated teacher when that person looks in the mirror. I will say more about this later in the chapter. What's important to know now is that I chose this chapter title because it uses language that struggling literacy coaches often use. Therefore, I think this title will best help readers to know what is in this chapter and with what problem this chapter will provide help.

So, let's get back to those three questions from the end of chapter 4, which are questions that typically are asked when I suggest that literacy coaches respond to teachers' own goals:

- What if a teacher has poor goals?
- What if a teacher has no goals?
- What if a teacher is resistant to my support?

In such situations, literacy coaches are attempting to understand the needs and concerns of individual teachers or teams of teachers. Once teachers, with assistance as needed from literacy coaches, have identified these needs and concerns, then they can prioritize them and establish goals for the most pressing ones. The teacher and coach then can develop a plan of action together.

What If a Teacher Has Poor Goals?

Distinguishing Poor Goals From Different Goals

Look as honestly as possible at your response to a teacher's poor goals, and ask yourself, Are the teacher's goals *poor*, or are they merely *different* from my own? This is a tough question. If you are passionate about teaching and reading, you surely feel strongly about the beliefs you hold, and, therefore, you know that you are right. I'm the same way. But as I continue to grow, I find that most often when I don't want to consider ideas that compete with mine, I am motivated by fear. I'm fearful that the ideas I've dismissed just might have merit, even just a little bit of merit, and this doesn't feel good.

We humans are sense-making beings. Our brains work hard to make sense of our world. If we think we have figured something out, especially something as important to us as teaching and learning, we want to hang on to it. We don't want to have our sense making disrupted by a competing view. In fact, there is a theory of brain organization that suggests that the oldest part of our brains (in evolutionary terms) encourages us to divide the world into two groups—(1) those like us and (2) those not like us (MacLean, 1990). The first group is the group we like and affiliate with; the other group is threatening to us and we want to reject it. (You can see how this skill was essential for survival at one time. It was important for our ancestors to be able to distinguish those not like us—for example, tigers—from those like us, in order to avoid getting eaten. However, this same survival skill leads to problems today, when this fine-tuned skill often leads to prejudice as we distinguish those not like us—for example, those who have different beliefs about teaching or even about religion—from those like us.) From this perspective, considering the worth of a teacher's competing views is not only threatening to the sense we've made of teaching and learning, it's threatening to our sense of how we fit into our world.

So, your first difficult task is to open your mind just a little bit further to allow that this teacher's goal may be different from yours but still worth considering. Your way of opening your mind may be different from mine, but my ability to consider others' perspectives from a less-rigid position has grown as my sense of self, my psychological centeredness, and my spirituality have grown. I encourage you to find your own ways to have a more open mind.

Of course, if you find that you and the teacher have differing but perfectly acceptable goals, you still have a problem, but it's less serious. Disagreeing with a goal is easier than believing that a goal is without merit. In the case of disagreeing with the goal, you will want to try to change your perceptions to understand the teacher's goal and assist the teacher; in the case of finding the goal without merit, you'll probably want to change the *teacher's* perceptions.

Considering the former option, how do you deal with a teacher's goal that has merit but is different from your own? Here are my suggestions.

1. *Don't try to pretend.* You will not further a trusting relationship if you pretend that you agree with a goal when you really don't. If the teacher is at all familiar with your work and your values, he or she will know that you don't agree and are pretending to. Even if the teacher doesn't know your work, at some point he or she may find out that you don't agree, and the teacher will feel betrayed if you have pretended to agree up to that point. This doesn't mean that you should state your disagreement outright or even that you should say anything about your views. You might do so if you have a long-term and very trusting relationship with the teacher, but most often you won't. In the latter case, your language should be much more neutral. For instance, you might say, "It sounds as if you have several reasons for making that decision," rather than "What a great idea!"

2. *Listen and learn.* Find out why the teacher has set the goal. Use prompts and questions such as, (a) Tell me more about that, (b) What made you decide on this goal? and (c) What will be different about your students upon implementation of this goal? However, here's the challenge: You need to ask these questions with a truly inquiring mind. If you are asking with a judging mind, I can almost guarantee that your judgmental stance will be revealed in subtle changes in your voice.

3. *Establish your respect for the teacher's perspective and goal.* Use language to make sure that the teacher knows you heard him or her. You might even restate the goal and the teacher's reasons for wanting to implement it.

4. *When you are successful in establishing a listening stance and in understanding the teacher's perspective, then you need to make a decision about whether you can comfortably work with the teacher.* If you find the teacher's goal so different from your own that you have trouble supporting it, you may want to refer the teacher to other sources for help. If you have been truly respectful and the teacher believes that you have heard and understood him or her, it may be comfortable to both of you if you state,

> Your goals sound well-thought-out, and I understand that they are important to you. However, I'm not coming from the same perspective so I probably can't help you as much as others could. Could I find another source of support for you?

Such alternate support might come from another teacher; another literacy coach; a workshop; or print, video, or online resources.

If you find that although you do not share the teacher's goals, you can support them, then proceed as usual with your best literacy coaching practices. At this stage, you also might raise alternate views, but only if you think they will be helpful to the teacher. In other words, raise alternate views to add useful information, not to argue your point.

An example may be useful. What follows is a scenario in which the literacy coach disagrees with teachers' goals but then finds that they have merit.

● ● ● ● ●

Maria is a literacy coach working with a group of fifth-grade teachers in an elementary school setting. These teachers have always taught in self-contained classrooms but have set a goal of moving to a departmentalized approach in which each teacher will be responsible for one core subject: reading, science, social studies, or math. Writing will be taught across the curriculum. Maria thinks this is a poor idea because she believes in integrating the content areas with reading instruction as well as writing instruction, and she doesn't see that being possible with this departmentalized approach. She recognizes her negative response to the teachers' idea and decides to set it aside until she learns more.

"Tell me more about your decision to departmentalize," Maria says at her first meeting with the fifth-grade teachers.

"Well," begins Paul, "we have noticed that we short-change the content areas of science and social studies. We think by making me entirely responsible for social studies and Leslie entirely responsible for science, we'll be sure to teach all the subjects as necessary."

"Also," chimes in Dorothy, "Paul is the only male teacher at the fifth-grade level, and we think all the students will benefit from an opportunity to interact with him. At this age, the boys are really looking for male role models."

Maria responds, "I see. You want to departmentalize in order to give all subjects adequate time and also to enable all students to interact with Paul. Have you looked at any other options?"

"We have," explains Leslie. "We visited Turner Elementary, over in Edgewater School District, where they use an integrated curriculum approach. We loved it, but we don't think it will work here because we don't have enough time to plan together. Also, Turner has a great library and an excellent computer lab, so they have resources for inquiry projects that we don't."

"So," replies Maria, "you'd find an integrated curriculum exciting but don't think it will work here due to lack of time and materials."

"Yes," the four teachers respond.

"Well, as you know, I worked with an integrated curriculum when I taught over at Jefferson Elementary, and, like you, I thought it was great. But I understand that you don't think it's workable here. I support your decision to move ahead with departmentalization, but I'm wondering.... Would it be beneficial to look at aspects of the Turner Elementary program that you liked and see if we can think creatively about how to include them in a departmentalized program? That may or may not be possible, but I'd be happy to help you explore possibilities."

In this example, Maria listens and learns, and then she responds with support. Even though she doesn't agree with the teachers' decision, she recognizes that it is well-thought-out, and she decides to assist them in whatever way she can. She also uses a good coaching skill called "*and*, not *or*." In other words, she suggests that there may be a choice that enables the teachers to departmentalize *and* include some of the aspects of the integrated curriculum used at Turner Elementary. By doing so, she helps the teachers think of greater possibilities.

All literacy coaches can use strategies similar to Maria's. By listening, learning, asking careful questions, and keeping an open mind, literacy coaches can assist teachers even when their goals are different from the coaches'. And in cases where such assistance is not possible because the teachers' goals are too contradictory of the coaches', literacy coaches who have established respectful relationships can sincerely suggest that teachers turn to others for assistance.

Identifying Poor Goals

Let's define "poor." A poor goal violates ethical principles (such as treating all students fairly), leads to student failure based upon carefully reviewed data, is inappropriate for the students in that particular classroom, or contradicts sound research. In regard to this latter item, be careful to know your research and what it does and doesn't say. Educators today make numerous claims about research, particularly in light of the federal government's emphasis on scientifically based research, and as a literacy coach, you will gain respect if you can discuss research with understanding and insight.

Indeed, there are goals that teachers set that can only be described as poor. A few from my own experience come to mind. For example, I once visited a classroom where the children's desks were in an outward-facing circle on a permanent basis, which meant the children did not interact with or even see each other for hours at a time. I also knew a teacher who divided her classroom library into "boys' books" and "girls' books" and separated the books according to stereotypical norms so, for instance, girls did not have the opportunity to read books about sports or wild animals, although they were given the books on household pets. And there are still far too many classrooms in which children are given punishments that involve writing the same sentence over and over again—often hundreds of times—and then the teachers wonder why the children aren't interested in writing.

If you are working with a teacher who selects a poor goal, I'd encourage you to take the following steps:

1. *Listen and learn.* As in the case of a teacher having a goal different from yours, when dealing with what appears to be a poor goal begin by listening to the teacher and learning his or her reasons for choosing that goal. You may be surprised to find some heartfelt and well thought-out reasoning. Often, you will find that you and the teacher share more in common than you might have guessed but choose different ways to reach the goal. For instance, teachers who group students by ability and those who don't usually share a goal of helping all students achieve but disagree about how to meet that goal and what gets in the way of accomplishing it. When there is a common outcome, there is more room for discussion. Although you and the teacher may not share the same short-term goal, you may be able to discuss long-term goals that you do have in common and find some common ground for working toward them.

2. *Be sure the teacher knows that you hear his or her reasons and honor his or her desired outcome.* It is unlikely that you'll hear from the teacher that he or she wants the students to fail or to be treated unfairly. Make sure that you and the teacher establish that you are both working for the success and well-being of the students.

3. *Honestly, but gently, express your reservations.* This is the tricky part. You might use one or more of the following strategies for this step:

(a) Cite an outside source. You might say something such as, "You know, this discussion makes me think of something I just read about a teacher who was trying the same thing. Can I look back at that and get back to you tomorrow about what she found?" If the teacher agrees, do just as you promised. Find the article or book and share the portion you mentioned with the teacher on the next day. Be careful not to put pressure on the teacher to agree with what the piece says. You might want to merely give the selected portion to the teacher and ask to discuss it at your next meeting. In that way, the teacher will have time to read and consider it on his or her own before discussing it with you.

(b) Share your experience. You might say something such as, "I had the same concern when I taught third grade. I tried something very similar and was so surprised by what I found. There was an unexpected result." Explain the result and then leave some time for the teacher to reflect before responding. You might say, "I'm not trying to get you to agree with me, but could I ask that you think about whether the same thing might happen in your situation? Maybe we could talk about it some more next week?"

(c) State a reservation. This is where you need to use your most neutral tone of voice and your friendliest—but least condescending—expression. You might proceed by stating, "I value your goal, but I wonder if there might be some unintended consequences. I'm concerned that the students will get unequal opportunities to learn with this approach."

4. *Ask what the goal will look like if implemented successfully.* This tactic accomplishes two purposes: First, it gets the teacher to move beyond the plan to the effect of the plan. Sometimes at this point the teacher realizes that it won't have the result that he or she intends. Second, if the teacher does go ahead with the goal, it gives you a criterion by which to gauge the goal's effectiveness.

5. *Ask the teacher to brainstorm other options, if possible.* By this point, the teacher probably will have concluded that you are not fond of his or her goal, and you may be pushing too hard to ask the teacher to consider other options, but do so if you can. Otherwise, consider asking the teacher if you could look at the professional literature to see how other teachers have approached the desired outcome, to see if there are other options available.

6. *Approach the teacher's supervisor.* If the teacher proceeds with his or her plan and you know it treats students inequitably or will cause their failure, you have a moral obligation to approach a supervisor about it. Clearly, this will compromise your position with that teacher and perhaps with some others on the staff, but you cannot stand by and watch children being treated inappropriately. If you discuss the matter with a supervisor, ask him or her to work with you to brainstorm ways to distance you from the process. *Use this step only when you have no choice, but do use it if necessary.*

Figure 4
Communication Strategies for Addressing Poor Goals

• • •

- ● Keep eye contact direct but friendly.

- ● Use a neutral tone of voice, devoid of judgment, cajoling, or condescension.

- ● Seek shared viewpoints and desired outcomes.

- ● Turn your shoulders toward the teacher, and uncross your legs and arms.

- ● State your "concerns," "options," or "perspectives," rather than "criticisms," "opinions," or "proof."

Regardless of your approach, use the communication tactics in Figure 4 for the best results.

Let's look at an example of how a literacy coach might successfully address a teacher who has a poor goal.

● ● ● ● ●

Donald is a literacy coach working with Alison, a first-grade teacher in a school in which the children come from low-income families who have recently moved to the United States. Most families come from Mexico, but a small group come from Russia. In virtually all cases, the children's parents speak English as a second language, but neither Donald nor Alison knows how capable the parents are in reading printed English. Alison recently attended a workshop in which the teachers in a suburban elementary school assigned all children the daily homework of reading with their parents for 15 minutes every evening. The school's test scores rose, and Alison returned to her school excited about implementing the same goal. In a conference, she shares the goal with Donald, who replies, "Wow, I hear your excitement about this reading homework program. Tell me more."

Alison responds, "The teachers at Oak Village School saw their test scores go up when they used it there. The kids read three times more books, and you know kids have to practice the skills and strategies they're learning."

"Boy, you're on target about the need to practice. I agree. How would you implement that goal here in your classroom?" Donald asks.

"I'd do the same thing," explains Alison. "My students would have a sheet that went home every Wednesday in the take-home folder, and they'd return it the following Tuesday. Parents would record the number of minutes they read with their children. Because these are first graders, the students could read to their parents or could listen to their parents read."

Donald believes that Alison's plan is unethical because there is not an adequate supply of books for children whose parents do not speak English. He responds, "I wonder how the parents who don't read English would fare. Do we have enough books written in Spanish or Russian for them to be able to read to their kids?"

Alison responds, "I've thought about that. Most of these parents know English, and the children need to learn to read in English. If the parents can't read to the children, then those children will have to read to the parents. Maybe the parents can learn along with their children."

Donald replies thoughtfully, "I hear you that you want the children to read in English. I wonder what the research says about the best way to get them to practice at home. Would it be OK if I looked around a little bit and shared with you what I found? Maybe there are some modifications we could make to particularly address this unique problem."

"Well," says Alison warily, "I'd hate to mess around with a program that worked so well."

"Yes, we don't want to spoil a good thing," says Donald. "But perhaps there's a way we can add value. We have a unique group of students here, and it would be exciting if we can take a good program and make it excellent for our students' own needs."

"Sure," Alison says. "Let me know how I can make the program fit these students' needs."

OK, this conversation may seem too ideal to you. If the conversation doesn't quite sound like one you would have, please bear with me. I believe the ideas behind it—the use of good communication skills, seeking to add value ("*and*, not *or*"), and honoring a teacher's goals—all have merit, even if the script is a little stilted. All literacy coaches can use similar strategies when working with teachers who have poor goals.

In this section, I've divided teachers' goals into "good but different" and "poor." By implication, there also are "good" teacher goals. All these labels are judgments that are tricky and that you should make with caution. It is always best to listen and learn before labeling and to try to be open to changing your judgment over time. In addition, try to live with a less-than-ideal goal before you dismiss it. It is always easier to go back to a teacher and say, "You know, after thinking about our discussion and doing some reading, I wonder if we could revisit your goal," than dismissing a goal outright and then trying to start the conversation again.

What If a Teacher Has No Goals?

Sometimes you'll attempt a coaching relationship with a teacher who says he or she has no goals. The teacher tells you that he or she likes the way things are going in the classroom and wishes you well in your work with the other teachers. In this case, one of two things may be happening: (1) The teacher may be resisting (if this is the case, you'll find valuable suggestions in the next section), or (2) the teacher may have goals but either may be incapable of recognizing them or hesitant to share them.

So, if the teacher does have goals but isn't recognizing them or telling you about them, what can you do? I recommend a carefully worded question, which I've mentioned previously:

> When you think of the kind of readers and writers you want your students to be and when you think about the kind of teaching you want to do, and when you think of the kind of classroom you want to have, what gets in the way?

The reason I like this question is because it assumes that all teachers have a vision of the kind of literate learners they want to have, the kind of teaching they want to do, and the kind of classrooms they want to have. I've never found a teacher who couldn't answer this question. Sometimes, actually more often than I'd like, the "what" that gets in the way is something outside the teacher's control (at least in the immediate sense), such as the school day schedule, the district curriculum, or the lack of breakfast some students experience. However, these obstacles get the teacher talking and provide an opening for the literacy coach.

If the teacher raises concerns beyond his or her control, you as the literacy coach might respond by asking what effect those obstacles have on the students' classroom performance. After listening, acknowledge the teacher's concerns and the negative effects such conditions have on the classroom.

Then, offer to assist in seeking ways to respond to those conditions, even if neither you nor the teacher can change them. (In addition, you may want to make a note to gently prod the school staff to address those concerns as a group. For instance, although an individual teacher cannot address limitations of the school day schedule, an entire staff might brainstorm ways to adjust the schedule or the way staff members are used during the day.) Here's an example of how one coach helped teachers respond to conditions outside their control.

● ● ● ● ●

Delia, a literacy coach in a middle school, is meeting with a team of eighth-grade teachers to whom she poses the key question: "When you think about the kind of readers and writers you want your students to be, and the kind of teaching you want to do, and the kind of classrooms you want to have, what gets in the way?"

"Time," Dave immediately responds. "We can't do it all in a 45-minute time period."

"Yes," agrees Consuela. "And the kids are absent so much, so we have even less time with them."

"But there's nothing we can do about that," adds Monica, "so we just do our best."

"I hear you," says Delia. "Time is a big factor. If we don't have time with the kids, we can't teach them much. Have you tried anything to address this problem?"

Dave's answer is a bit cantankerous: "We can't control the school schedule. The school board sets that up. And we can't get the kids to school. I report the kids who are frequently absent to the Dean, but he's so overworked that he never gets around to them."

"I know that these are not things you can control directly," replies Delia, while making a note to mention attendance concerns to the principal as a topic for discussion at a staff meeting. "But they clearly affect your classroom. How would you feel if I could help you find some ways to make teaching easier under such conditions?"

"No offense," Consuela says, "but we've been at this a long time. I'm not sure what you could do to fix it."

"Oh, I agree, I can't fix it," responds Delia. "My offer is to work with you to see if we can pool our ideas—and maybe I can access some resources—to make living with the problem a bit easier. I know you are great teachers and have a great deal of experience. What I have to offer is a little time to look at the professional literature on time use, and I also could request some substitutes so we could spend an entire morning working on this problem. Maybe we could visit another school or attend a workshop. None of these efforts will necessarily provide <u>the</u> solution, but perhaps they'll give us some small ideas worth considering."

"Well, I'm doubtful that there's anything we haven't thought of," Dave replies. "But if you want to give it a shot, I guess we've got nothing to lose."

And thus, Delia has started a coaching relationship. She has begun a conversation that might, over a period of several years, lead to a number of goals for this group of teachers and a greater sense of effectiveness and influence among them all. All literacy coaches can use strategies such as these to ask key questions, listen carefully, rephrase what was heard, and focus teachers' attention. In these ways, individuals or groups who appear to have no goals can be assisted in developing some.

What If a Teacher Is Resistant to My Support?

The number one concern of literacy coaches is the resistant teacher, which is no surprise. If literacy coaches are in the business of helping teachers change, the most difficult part of the job naturally is those people who won't let the coaches do their jobs. Resistant teachers are different from teachers who have no goals or don't want to share their goals. Resistant teachers simply don't want to participate in the literacy coaching process.

What Is Resistance?

Let's reconsider what resistance means before suggesting ways for literacy coaches to work with it. Resistance is typically thought of as a negative behavior. Those teachers who resist are "poor" teachers. But let's reconsider that notion. Think about when you've resisted an initiative, whether at work, at home, in your community, or anyplace else. Why did you resist? I bet it was because you believed you were right on moral or intellectual grounds. You just *knew* that the idea was ill formed, you knew of research that demonstrated its weakness, or you were sure it was amoral or harmful. When we ourselves resist, we believe it is because we are good people who care about our work, communities, homes, and institutions. But when others resist, we often believe they are lazy, unconcerned, uninformed, or difficult. In other words, resistance is good in the eyes of the resister, bad in the eyes of those being resisted.

With this concept in mind, let's agree to make no judgments about the character of those who resist. Resisters are not inherently bad, even when they are resisting us. In the field of psychoanalysis, where the term *resistance* is commonly used, there is an understanding that resistance is a tool for growth. By examining why a person resists, one can learn more about that person's fears and motivations, the influence of the person's past, and the effect of the relationship with the analyst. In the process, growth occurs. This approach to resistance may be useful to literacy coaches as well, although I am not suggesting that literacy coaches act as psychoanalysts.

Having established that teachers who resist literacy coaches are not necessarily bad or ill motivated, and their resistance actually might be a source of information and growth, how do literacy coaches work from this perspective? The first step always should be to listen and learn. Table 8 includes some common statements made by resistant teachers, some possible reasons for those statements, and some suggested responses that literacy coaches might make.

Should I "Waste Time" Working With Resisters?

There's an adage in professional development circles that one should not waste one's time with resisters. I used to agree but have changed my mind. Literacy coaches can learn so much from resisters. First, literacy coaches can learn more about why teachers disagree with the literacy coaching model. This will help the coaches to either better explain themselves or to try new approaches to the role of literacy coach. Second, in cases where teachers are resistant to literacy coaches' approaches to literacy or instruction, the coaches can learn other perspectives and, even if they don't agree with these perspectives, can attempt to see what they're doing through other lenses. Third, literacy coaches can learn what the resisting teachers value, which usually reduces the distance among a resisting teacher and a literacy coach and other teachers because they understand one another better and may find shared values among themselves.

Let me give an example from my own experience. I was working with a school staff that was debating the best approach to spelling instruction. The staff was divided between those who wanted to continue to use the traditional spelling program based on a spelling workbook and those who wanted to teach spelling based on words encountered in the content areas and in the children's own writing. After debating instructional methods and materials—both formally at a staff meeting and informally in after-

Table 8
Responding to Resistant Teachers

• • •

Teacher's Statement	Possible Motivations for Teacher's Statement	Literacy Coach's Response
"Sorry, but I just don't have time for this."	● The teacher does not have time. ● The teacher wants the literacy coach to go away.	● "I understand. When would be a good time for me to come back?"
"There's nothing I need help with."	● The teacher does not recognize any goals. ● The teacher wants the literacy coach to go away.	● Use The Question ● "I'd like to learn about your work for my own sake. Because I work with everyone in the school, it's helpful for me to know where our strengths are as much as where our problems are. Can we talk about your classroom?" Then ask the key question.
"I've been around for a long time. There's nothing you can teach me."	● The teacher has had previous negative experiences with literacy coaches and other "professional developers." ● The teacher wants the literacy coach to go away.	● "I hear you. That's why my role is not to teach you new things. It's to support you as you work toward your goals." Then ask the key question. ● "You probably have some things you could teach some of the new teachers around here. Could I learn more about your classroom so I can share what you're doing with others?"

school hallway conversations—the staff and I sat down to discuss their and my beliefs about spelling instruction.

This discussion led to our realization that we had many of the same beliefs. Where we disagreed was in how to implement those beliefs. We also learned the source of some individuals' strong support for one or the other approach. In one case, a teacher wept as she told the group of her own son's struggle to spell and of her belief that elimination of the spelling workbooks would lead other students to experience the same kind of struggle. The outcome of all of this sharing was that members of each side of the debate had greater understanding of the motivations held by those they were seeing as resisters, and we agreed to a statement of principle about what we *all* valued in spelling instruction.

When we listen to and learn from resisters, the conversation is richer, the differences often are blurred, and we usually can honor one another as people and teachers even if we still disagree.

I believe the notion of not wasting time on resisters was actually developed in response to the amount of attention a negative teacher can consume from someone such as a literacy coach. For instance, if a literacy coach selects one teacher who is very resistant as the measure of his or her success, the coach may spend an inordinate amount of time trying to change that teacher, which will lead to frustration and a lack of time for the other teachers. So the idea of not wasting time might be rephrased as, "Don't let a resisting teacher consume all of your time and energy." *Do* spend time listening to and learning from that teacher, but don't consider that teacher as the gauge of whether you've been successful or not.

Conclusion

When those of us who teach started out in the profession, we had an idea of what it would be like to have our own classrooms. Most of us pictured ideal situations, with ideal students. We believed that even the so-called difficult kids would quickly come around when they were met by our skill, intelligence, and charm. For most new teachers, however, there is a period of dismay when faced with children as they really are. In a similar manner, many literacy coaches wish for certain kinds of teachers to work with, and they feel dismay when the teachers with whom they must work are not what they expected or preferred. Figure 5 represents the kinds of teachers with whom literacy coaches struggle and the coaching tasks that may be used in response.

It is essential for literacy coaches to have in their toolkits the skills for recognizing the reasons why teachers make literacy coaches unhappy, uncomfortable, or unsuccessful. In addition, literacy coaches need skills in relating to teachers with open minds, in order to learn about teachers' perspectives and respond appropriately. By recognizing teachers with different goals, poor goals, or no goals, and by preparing for teachers who appear

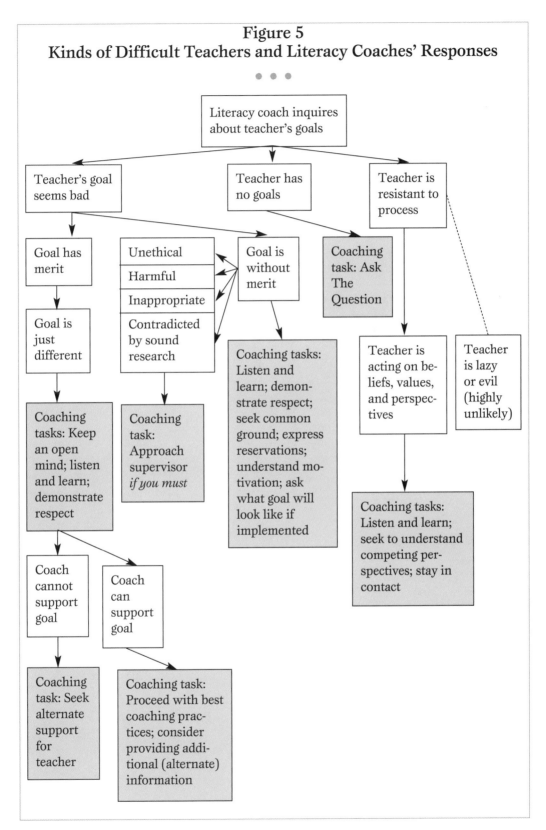

Figure 5
Kinds of Difficult Teachers and Literacy Coaches' Responses

● ● ●

Literacy coach inquires about teacher's goals

Teacher's goal seems bad

Teacher has no goals

Teacher is resistant to process

Goal has merit

Unethical

Harmful

Inappropriate

Contradicted by sound research

Goal is without merit

Coaching task: Ask The Question

Teacher is lazy or evil (highly unlikely)

Goal is just different

Coaching tasks: Keep an open mind; listen and learn; demonstrate respect

Coaching task: Approach supervisor *if you must*

Coaching tasks: Listen and learn; demonstrate respect; seek common ground; express reservations; understand motivation; ask what goal will look like if implemented

Teacher is acting on beliefs, values, and perspectives

Coach cannot support goal

Coach can support goal

Coaching tasks: Listen and learn; seek to understand competing perspectives; stay in contact

Coaching task: Seek alternate support for teacher

Coaching task: Proceed with best coaching practices; consider providing additional (alternate) information resistant, literacy coaches can optimize their chances for influencing change in their schools.

In this chapter, I have attempted to identify the most difficult challenges in the work done by literacy coaches. At this point in the book, I have identified many of the skills and strategies used by successful literacy coaches. However, I suspect that readers may still have some questions. In the following chapter, I address miscellaneous issues and concerns that are often raised by literacy coaches.

ADDITIONAL RESOURCES FOR LITERACY COACHES

de Dreu, C.K.W., & de Vries, N.K. (1997). Minority dissent in organizations. In C.K.W. de Dreu & E. Van de Vliert (Eds.), *Using conflict in organizations* (pp. 72–86). Thousand Oaks, CA: Sage.

DiPardo, A. (1997). Of war, doom, and laughter: Images of collaboration in the public-school workplace. *Teacher Education Quarterly, 24*(1), 89–104.

Evans, S., & Cohen, S.S. (2000). *Hot buttons: How to resolve conflict and cool everyone down.* New York: Cliff Street.

Stone, D., Patton, B., & Heen, S. (1999). *Difficult conversations: How to discuss what matters most.* New York: Viking.

CHAPTER 9

What About __This__ Issue?

- What should I do when a teacher refuses my assistance?

- How should I respond to pressure from my principal to raise test scores?

- Are there times when I should choose a teacher's goals for him or her?

- Should I ever tell a teacher what to do?

- How do I manage a teaching assignment <u>plus</u> a literacy coaching job?

- How can I make teachers comfortable with me in their classrooms?

- Am I supposed to have a debriefing meeting after a demonstration lesson?

- What should I do if I am asked to lead a professional development workshop?

- How do I respond when asked to evaluate a student?

- How can I respond to teachers who believe that "those kids"—usually groups underrepresented in our school— simply won't or can't learn?

- How do I know if I'm doing a good job?

As you near the end of this book, you may still have unanswered questions. This chapter attempts to answer the remaining questions you may have. There is some overlap between parts of this chapter and ideas presented in earlier chapters, and this is intentional. I find when working with literacy coaches that they often need to be reminded several times of some specific principles of coaching. I have structured this chapter differently than the previous chapters because the content of this chapter comes as a result of follow-up questions literacy coaches have asked me after I've been working with them for a while. The chapter consists of those questions with the answers I provide.

1. *I work with a teacher who keeps telling me I'm doing a good job but she doesn't need any help from me. So far, I've just sort of ignored her. What do you advise?*
First, listen and learn. What is the teacher doing? What are her students doing, and how are they behaving? Is the teacher feeling relaxed or stressed at the end of the day? In other words, get more information to gauge why the teacher does not want to work with you. Then, use that information to decide your next step. If the teacher does not seem to be experiencing a great deal of stress and her students are doing well, try to develop a collaborative relationship in which you and others can learn from her. If the teacher is struggling, try to develop trust so you and she can begin to have a conversation. Once she seems to feel comfortable with you, ask the key question: When you think about the kind of reading and writing you want your students to do, the kind of literate lives you want students to have, the kind of classroom you want to have, the kind of teaching you want to be able to do, what gets in your way? Finally, remember that establishing a coaching relationship takes time: Don't ignore the teacher, but don't rush into anything.

2. *You write about letting teachers set goals and proceeding from that point, but my principal is putting pressure on me to raise test scores. What should I do?*
The coaching work described in this book will optimize the conditions for student achievement, so you and the principal should see eye to eye on methods if you are both aiming for improved achievement. (See the Introduction for a summary of research indicating that literacy coaching supports student achievement.) However, literacy coaching takes time, so the principal may not see the results as quickly as he or she would like. Start by listening to and learning from your principal. What does he or she expect you to be doing? What is his or her definition of literacy coaching? Does the principal have insight regarding what the test scores reflect?

Then, ask the principal to help you develop a plan. Are there grade levels or areas of literacy that he or she thinks you should emphasize most? Share what you think, too. For instance, can you show the principal data from the teachers with whom you are working that demonstrate the goals you are working on and the way those goals are supporting student achievement? If not, could you? What about looking at the alignment of the curriculum, the actual teaching that is taking place, and assessments? Could you and the principal lead the staff in aligning all aspects of the curriculum, instruction, and assessments and therefore increasing the chances that the assessments will accurately measure what is being taught?

There are a great many directions in which you could go within the literacy coaching model I've presented that probably would be reassuring to your principal. However, if you and the principal disagree on the role of a literacy coach or the manner in which you do your literacy coaching work, you may need to ask for some help. Invite the district coaching supervisor or someone else to assist you and the principal in redefining your work, reviewing your job description, or perhaps finding a position that better suits your vision. Now, here's the challenge: Can you do all that and still behave in a professional manner toward the principal?

3. *Is there ever a time when I should tell a teacher what goals to have?*
I'd advise against it. As soon as you take this "pushing" approach to coaching (i.e., telling the teacher what to do), you alter the relationship between the two of you significantly, putting yourself in a position of authority that will ultimately work against you. (For more on the concepts of coaches who "pull" or "push," see Eaton & Johnson, 2001.)

4. *According to your model of change, is there* ever *a time when a literacy coach should tell a teacher what to do or how to change?*
I'd suggest that timing and the nature of your relationship with the teacher are the factors to consider. In general, the longer you work with a teacher and the more that teacher and you have a trusting relationship, the more direct you can be with him or her. If you are not sure, you could ask the teacher by saying something such as, "You know, Jill, we've worked together for two years now, and I think we're pretty comfortable with each other. I have a suggestion that I'd like to make, but I don't want to disrupt our comfort level. What do you think?"

5. *My job requires me to work with students in a pull-out support program four hours a day in addition to literacy coaching. What should I do?*
Adjust your expectations for how much you can do as a literacy coach. It sounds like you have a half-time literacy coaching job. After you accept the limitations of that assignment, work with the staff and principal to understand these limitations. You might ask for some time at a faculty meeting to ask staff members to brainstorm all the things they'd like you to do. Then, ask their help in estimating how many hours a week each task would take. Finally, ask them to prioritize what they'd like you to do, given that you have 20 hours per week available.

6. *How do I get teachers comfortable with having me in their classrooms?*
First, you need to clarify for yourself and the teachers why you are in the classrooms. Honestly, if a teacher hasn't invited you into his or her classroom, you may not want to go. If a teacher does invite you, but then gets nervous when you arrive, say, to do a demonstration lesson, you should try to tolerate his or her nervousness for a bit and see if it subsides. One sure way to ease a teacher's discomfort is to make a mistake in your demonstration

lesson. (There's no need to plan that—you're human, so you'll make a mistake sooner or later, like the rest of us!) Then, in the debriefing session with the teacher, talk about the mistake and ask the teacher for feedback on what he or she saw.

Another way to begin working in a classroom is to read a story to the class. This is a fairly low-risk visit for the teacher and may get him or her used to your teaching style and your presence in the classroom.

7. So should I have a debriefing session after I do a demonstration lesson?
I'd recommend it. A debriefing session encourages a sense that you and the teacher are engaged in a collaborative conversation. It gives you a chance to think aloud about the decisions you made and why you made them. It also provides an opportunity for you to receive valuable feedback from a professional colleague. After the debriefing portion of the meeting, you may want to talk about the next steps: Will the teacher try the same thing on his or her own? Will you go back for a follow-up demonstration? Will you and the teacher co-plan a follow-up? Will you try something different?

8. You haven't talked about leading professional development workshops. How would I lead them?
You're right. I made a choice not to talk about leading professional development workshops because leading a large-group workshop is one of those gray areas of literacy coaching. It may support your literacy coaching work by providing whole-group information, discussion, or practice on a topic that you will then coach—a kind of workshop that fits entirely within the parameters of a literacy coach's work. On the other hand, a large-group workshop could be about a topic unrelated to your literacy coaching, and then it is not part of your literacy coaching work.

Most literacy coaches seem pretty comfortable with workshops. If you don't, you may want to start by using your good teaching practices just as you do with students. For instance, assess needs of the learners, develop goals, decide how you'll determine whether your goals are met, plan for interaction among participants, and get feedback before the workshop is over. Remember, too, that adult learners like to have some say in the content and format of their learning and like to see immediate applications. If you want assistance in leading workshops, you might start with the suggestions of the National Staff Development Council at www.nsdc.org.

9. What should I do if a teacher asks me to evaluate a student?
As in many cases, my first advice is to listen and learn. Find out why the teacher is interested in knowing more about this student and what the teacher already has tried. This may be an opportunity for you to coach the

teacher in developing a new assessment skill. On the other hand, this may be a chance for you to model how an educator can use assessment data to make instructional decisions, even if you are the one gathering all the data. (Use this approach if you think it would be too much to ask the teacher to learn new assessment practices at this point. For instance, the teacher may be very new and feel overwhelmed with all there is to learn, or the teacher may have a particularly difficult class and need a helping hand.) Sometimes, too, a teacher is looking for another professional opinion to support her assessments or observations. In all of these cases, I'd say, go ahead. However, if you find that you are getting a large number of requests for evaluations, you probably will want to consult with the principal and perhaps the staff about their priorities for your literacy coaching work. You also might lead a whole-staff workshop on easy assessment practices (e.g., checklists, inventories, and observation notes) and then invite teachers to participate in a more intensive series of workshops, practice sessions, and coaching support on in-process reading assessments such as running records, miscue analyses, or assessment rubrics for written work.

10. *A group of teachers at my school are convinced that "the problem" is "those kids." They use "those kids" to describe a cluster of economically disadvantaged African American students who attend this otherwise middle class white school. How can I respond?*

This situation is a tough one, and it occurs quite often for literacy coaches. Remember to listen and learn first. Then, you may share your own experience or understanding that economically disadvantaged African American children can be successful students.

Offer to help the teachers to figure out why this particular group of students is not succeeding. There are many articles in professional journals about helping children from all backgrounds succeed. Under the No Child Left Behind Act of 2001, your school must analyze the achievement of students in a variety of subgroups, including subgroups of students in major racial categories and children who are economically disadvantaged. Thus, you can remind teachers that they are expected by federal law to help all students achieve.

In addition, you may want to offer a study group on some of the research on what is often referred to as "the achievement gap" (Lee, 1998). The theories, studies, and beliefs presented in this research vary significantly, so it will be important for your group of teachers to take the time to look at a variety of claims and think carefully about what they are reading.

11. *How do I know if I'm doing a good job of coaching?*

Start at the microlevel and work through stages to the macrolevel. At the microlevel, evaluate how you feel about the work you are doing. Do you go to work feeling confident? Do you leave work at the end of the day with a sense of having accomplished something? Do you dread Monday mornings or look forward to them? You could use the self-assessment from *Coaching Successfully* (Eaton & Johnson, 2000, pp. 66–69) to evaluate your performance. This set of 32 questions provides an opportunity to rate oneself on a scale of 1 to 4. Be aware, however, that the tool is designed to be used by individuals in a variety of roles, including managers who use coaching as part of their supervisory process; therefore, some questions on the instrument may not apply to literacy coaches. Another source of reflection on your literacy coaching is provided by Lyons (2002, pp. 115–116). She encourages literacy coaches to reflect on whether they accomplished their goals as well as whether they helped the teacher accomplish her goal. From my perspective, these are one and the same, because a coach's goal should be to help meet the teacher's goal. Nonetheless, Lyons's ideas about reflecting after coaching are helpful. She stresses that good coaching is recognizable if one can ascertain that the teacher met her goal.

At the next level, you can get feedback from teachers and the principal of your school, and perhaps even parents of students in your school. These data could be collected informally, but you'll be more thorough if you conduct a survey or ask a neutral party to do some evaluative interviews. You also could ask for feedback from other literacy coaches in your district or from a district coaching supervisor. Then, look at and listen to what the teachers are doing and saying. Is the environment in the school any different because of your literacy coaching work?

At the macrolevel, monitor changes in student achievement. You and the rest of the staff are probably monitoring formal test scores. In addition, look at in-process reading inventories—such as running records and miscue analyses—gauge student motivation and out-of-school reading and writing, and look at the amount of time students read and write at school. If your school is using a range of literacy assessments, it should not be difficult to find such data. Of course, it is difficult to determine whether changes in student achievement can be attributed to literacy coaching. You could design a complex research study, but chances are you won't have the time or resources for that. Therefore, you may have to trust that if student assessments are positive, you've contributed to that progress. Don't take all the credit for it—of course, the credit goes to many—but enjoy the fact that as a building leader you surely are making a difference. If there is not change, or student assessments are negative, don't take all the responsibility, either. Pay attention to the data, reflect upon them with the rest of the staff, roll up your sleeves, and get back to work.

Conclusion

This chapter addresses additional questions that literacy coaches often ask. Of course, I can't list all possible questions here. Therefore, I encourage you to start with this book and then develop additional ways to get support for your questions and concerns. Turn to your principal, other literacy coaches, or a district-level coaching or curriculum supervisor. In addition, turn to professional organizations in order to develop a network of support.

However, even with a great deal of support, literacy coaching is difficult work. When I interact with literacy coaches, I frequently advise them to truly "take care." In other words, I recommend that they be vigilant about caring for themselves and doing whatever is necessary to help them survive the challenges of their work. The next chapter provides practical suggestions about these matters.

ADDITIONAL RESOURCES FOR TEACHERS

Compton-Lilly, C. (2004). *Confronting racism, poverty, and power: Classroom strategies to change the world*. Portsmouth, NH: Heinemann.

Shannon, P. (1998). *Reading poverty*. Portsmouth, NH: Heinemann.

Vogt, M., & Shearer, B.A. (2003). *Reading specialists in the real world: A sociocultural view*. Boston: Allyn & Bacon.

CHAPTER 10

How Do I Survive This Job?

- How can I manage all the tasks of literacy coaching?
- How do I prevent myself from getting discouraged?
- Is there any hope for making a difference?

T his chapter offers practices that literacy coaches can use to survive on the job. There is nothing unique about literacy coaching that would make the survival strategies different from those that you'd find for other stressful jobs. Nor is literacy coaching unique among people-related jobs in which being one's best directly influences the way one works with one's "clients."

Because most of the strategies in this chapter are familiar, I will review each rather briefly. This doesn't mean they are unimportant: I'd suggest ideas such as these are essential to literacy coaches, in fact. However, these ideas probably will serve more as reminders rather than new information for you.

Note Your Accomplishments

By the middle of the school year, many literacy coaches are wondering if their efforts are worth anything at all. They notice the teachers who have ignored their suggestions, they review student assessments that show great need, and they check their records and realize that there are a few teachers they haven't met with in months. Literacy coaches, like most people, are not satisfied until the job is finished. The difficult thing about literacy coaching, though, is that the job never is finished. If literacy coaches' work is to strengthen the ability of the staff to increasingly help their students achieve literacy success, then literacy coaches will always have something else to do.

In a way, literacy coaching success is like writing improvement: If we look at a single piece produced by a struggling writer, we may find our attention going to the flaws in expression, the confusing details, the poor punctuation, or other negative attributes of the writing. But if we look at the student's work over time, comparing a current piece of writing with ones done six months, one year, and two years ago, we probably will be amazed at the writer's progress and excited by many aspects of his or her current effort. It's all a matter of perspective. I encourage literacy coaches to take a parallel approach to their work in order to develop a parallel kind of perspective.

So, literacy coaches, please take a few minutes every week to note the things you have accomplished. You might begin team and individual meetings with such observations, too, so everyone in the school can acknowledge the hard work that they do. In addition, note where you started and where you are now. Begin every semester with a review of your progress. In other words, pay attention to your accomplishments, not only what has yet to be done.

Find a Support System

It is important to many people to have support systems, which is at least in part why we have friends, spouses, or partners, and why we stay in touch with family members and former classmates. I'd encourage literacy coaches to specifically nurture a support system of other literacy coaches or, if that's not possible, other educators in leadership positions. The key is that members of a literacy coach's professional support system should work outside of his or her school building. By developing support outside the school building, a literacy coach gains several advantages. First, the coach gets a more objective perspective than he or she would get from someone in the same school. Second, the coach increases the odds that what is said will remain confidential. Third, the coach avoids being seen as having "favorites" among the staff with whom he or she works. And fourth, the coach benefits from widening his or her horizons and hearing what is happening in other schools and perhaps other districts.

Finding a support system of teacher leaders from outside one's building is usually easy if one teaches in a large school district. However, in a smaller school district a literacy coach may have no counterparts. This is a good time to remember that the International Reading Association has active local councils throughout the United States, in Canada, and in many other countries. Also, the Internet can make literacy coaching collaboration possible across distances.

Focus on Feeling Centered

When I use the word *centered*, I'm referring to a sense that I get when I am focused on the moment at hand, grounded in what is going on right in front of me, and calmly poised to face whatever that is. Some people refer to it as "being in the zone." Many traditions of martial arts, athletics, or meditation place attention on the area of the solar plexus, just beneath one's belly button, as a location of solidness. Physiologically, this area is one's center of gravity when in a standing position. Psychologically, it can represent the core of one's sense of self. Spiritually, it can attune one to a source of energy, creativity, or being. Thus, you can think of being centered as important in a physiological, psychological, or spiritual dimension, depending on your personal beliefs.

I'd encourage you to focus on feeling centered as you engage in literacy coaching. You can do this by breathing in a way that allows your breath to go all the way down to the bottom of your lungs, causing the middle and lower parts of your torso to expand. Others prefer to engage in formal practices, such as yoga or qi gong, to help them become more centered. Still others find prayer of one kind or another will promote a calm feeling of being connected solidly with one's life and the spirit behind that life. (By suggesting these practices as a source of centering, I don't intend to downplay other purposes one might have for doing them.)

Find Ways to Relieve Stress

Methods for relieving stress are available to almost everyone these days. Articles in newspapers and magazines, reports on television, and pamphlets at doctors' offices all provide suggestions, including getting enough rest and exercise, talking about what's bothering you, having a support system, developing close relationships, making healthy food choices, and keeping a positive attitude. We know what to do to relieve stress, so how come so few of us do it? I can't answer that question, but I can encourage you to take the above suggestions seriously and try to incorporate stress relief into your daily life.

Don't Own All the Problems

Literacy coaches work in environments in which many factors are out of their control. Students come to school hungry, teachers work too many hours, parents lose their jobs, the school district goes into debt, cartoon violence shows its influence on the playground, and so much more. Sometimes it's easy for literacy coaches to get so caught up in their work that they forget that their failures are not always their failures.

Literacy coaches do important work, but that work is a small part of the education picture. When change is not occurring as literacy coaches wish, they should not give up and they should evaluate how they can do their work more effectively, but they should not take all the responsibility. My advice is to not feel responsible but to never stop trying.

Have Hope

My favorite survival tip for literacy coaches is to have hope. Literacy coaches try so hard and feel so much commitment, and they do sometimes wonder what it's all worth. My advice is to remember this: No matter how much you may disagree with other educators about teaching practices, class management, assessment, or anything else, what you have in common with them is that you all care about students. I really believe this. My career has given me the chance to work with thousands of teachers, and I have met only one who didn't care about children. (I'm pleased to tell you that she is no longer in the education field.) This is the source of my hope. As long as there are millions of adults going to work every day at least in part because they care about children, we can hope for anything. And this is where literacy coaches can be so important. When a literacy coach encourages a teacher by mirroring what teachers are doing—describing what he or she sees and hears a teacher doing successfully—and assuring that teacher that the teacher's work is of value, the odds increase that that teacher will continue to do work that demonstrates care for students and commitment to their success.

Conclusion

As literacy coaches struggle to do their jobs well, they would be wise to remember a few key survival strategies:

1. Remember to breathe.
2. Have hope.
3. See the good.
4. Take care of yourself.

Beyond these key survival strategies, literacy coaches would be wise to maintain perspective on their own goals and the parameters of their work. The conclusion provides an overview of what coaches should and shouldn't do.

ADDITIONAL RESOURCES FOR LITERACY COACHES

Palmer, P.J. (1998). *The courage to teach: Exploring the inner landscape of a teacher's life*. San Francisco: Jossey-Bass.
Sandholtz, K., Derr, B., Buckner, K., & Carlson, D. (2002). *Beyond juggling: Rebalancing your busy life*. Berkeley, CA: Berrett-Koehler.

What Do Coaches Do?
What Don't They Do?

- What do literacy coaches do?
- What don't literacy coaches do?
- What are some good questioning practices?
- How do I go about mirroring?
- How do I avoid taking on supervisory duties?
- Why is it harmful to judge teachers, and how can I avoid doing so?
- Should I observe teachers in their classrooms?

I've debated with myself whether this chapter should go at the beginning or the end of the book. I decided to place it at the end for two reasons: (1) I want it to serve as a review of important duties for literacy coaches, and (2) I want it to be an inspiration as readers proceed with their literacy coaching work.

As the chapter title indicates, I've divided literacy coaches' duties into what they do and what they don't do. Therefore, for ease, I've also divided the chapter according to those two categories. The first part of the chapter discusses what coaches do, the latter part provides what coaches don't do.

What Literacy Coaches Do

Listen

If you've read all the previous chapters, you've noticed that I mention listening a great deal. When you're in doubt about what to do as a literacy coach, listen. In fact, listening is especially important when you don't know what to do because your hesitation is probably a sign that you need more information. In my personal and professional lives, I've never heard anyone criticized or disliked because he or she listened too carefully.

Ask Questions

If you doubt yourself as a literacy coach because you don't feel that you have enough expertise, then develop expertise in this one area: asking good questions. A good cue that you need to ask questions is when you have an uncomfortable feeling of being put on the spot by someone else. Clearly, at that moment, you don't feel ready to reply, so ask questions. If you are feeling put on the spot because you don't know how to reply to the person, asking more questions buys you some time and helps you narrow the issue, perhaps to something you can answer. If you are feeling put on the spot because you think you are being set up (as when a teacher asks, "What do you think about the basal series we just adopted?"), asking more questions can help you understand the concern that is behind the issue raised. And if you are feeling put on the spot because the person's request was completely unexpected, inquiring further can allow you to understand the other person's thinking and perhaps even see how it connects to the topic at hand.

We all assume that we know how to ask questions, and I suppose we do to some degree. But the following types of questions seem more useful than others:

- Open-ended questions—those without a yes or no answer—usually are helpful because they encourage teachers to provide more information.

- Questions that leave room for a range of reflection are good in a group discussion. For instance, asking a study group, "What struck you as most useful for your teaching?" will produce more reflection than asking, "Do you think that the book's suggestions on revision would work in your classroom?"

- Questions are best when they do not leave a person feeling put on the spot. For example, when a teacher says that he or she tried a practice and it didn't work, that person might feel attacked if you say, "What's your proof?" However, he or she may feel more comfortable if you ask, "What did you notice as you were trying it?" (See chapter 5 for additional suggestions.)

Mirror the Teacher's Words or Actions

A literacy coach can play a valuable role by telling a teacher what the coach sees. In other words, the literacy coach serves as a mirror for the teacher. For example, Deborah, a literacy coach, meets individually with Wes, a sixth-grade teacher. Wes bursts into the room. "I've had it!" he declares. "I've tried everything to get the kids to write. I've given them topics and let them pick. I've shown them dozens of examples of good writing. I've brought in an author and a journalist. I've let them do projects that they write about. I've let them write notes to each other. Nothing—nothing—works." Deborah responds as a mirror and says, "You're really frustrated. You've worked so hard to promote writing, and your students are not interested."

In this example, mirroring takes the form of active listening. In other words, Deborah repeats what she heard Wes say, to make clear that she has heard him. Sometimes, however, mirroring provides reflection of what a teacher is doing, not saying. For instance, when a teacher has totally revamped his or her reading workshop time, it can be valuable for the literacy coach to serve as a mirror and note all of the things the teacher has done. Such mirroring assures the teacher that his or her efforts are not going unnoticed and also reminds the teacher of just how much work he or she has done.

I find that mirroring is especially valued by teachers now, when so much of the public feedback they receive is negative. Teachers so often read in the newspaper and hear on television that they are not doing their jobs effectively and that others could do it better. It is important for those who support teachers, including literacy coaches, to mirror the teachers' efforts and their investment in their work.

Collect Data

Literacy coaches need to collect data at three levels. First, they need to be part of the team that looks at schoolwide data on literacy achievement. Certainly, this includes test scores, but it also includes data on use of the library, parent participation in literacy-related activities, professional development in literacy, and other evidence of a literacy-learning culture. Second, literacy coaches need to collect data on their own work. How do they know they are making a difference? How do they know that their practices are effective? Data collection will assist in answering these important questions. Third, literacy coaches should sometimes assist teachers in collecting data. This is a tricky issue because some teachers may prefer that the literacy coaches be responsible for data collection related to those teachers' classrooms. However, this is inappropriate because collecting and using data is an essential part of effective teaching, and teachers need to know how to do it themselves. Rather, the literacy coach should assist the teacher in planning for data collection and analyzing data, and the literacy coach may occasionally do the actual data collection when it is impossible for the teacher to do so. For instance, if a teacher would like to gauge students' on-task behavior during reading workshop, when he or she is busy with guided reading groups, the literacy coach may come to the classroom and collect data about student activity at five-minute intervals throughout the workshop time.

Provide Resources

When literacy coaches provide resources—such as books, teaching aids, professional articles, and computer software—they are not actually providing for substantial change. However, they may indeed be creating potential for deeper changes. In other words, by helping teachers to have the resources they need—and by saving teachers the time needed to track down those resources—literacy coaches help teachers get ready to try new alternatives, which can be valuable in and of itself.

However, providing resources appears to be some of the best public relations literacy coaches can have. Perhaps because resources are visible and concrete, and because they are often in short supply in schools, they remind teachers of the valuable service that literacy coaches can provide. Most literacy coaches have at least one story about a teacher with whom they were not successfully making a connection, until the coach found some material resources for the teacher. That effort subsequently led to a deeper connection and more collaboration between teacher and coach.

Coaches perform a range of duties that support their key clients—teachers. Some of these duties, such as listening, questioning, and mirroring, require strong skills in relating to others. On the other hand, some of these duties, such as providing resources and collecting data, require content-related skills. Both sets of "do's" reflect the need for literacy coaches to be well versed in the process and content of their work, and to continue to update and refine their skills as they proceed.

What Literacy Coaches Don't Do

Supervise

Literacy coaches who get pulled into supervisory duties will never have the trust of the teachers with whom they work. Teachers won't open up to a literacy coach if the coach's work in any way influences the teachers' performance reviews. However, despite the indisputable truth of this statement, literacy coaches often find themselves on the edge of supervisory roles. This occurs most often in one of two ways.

Sometimes, literacy coaches themselves are so upset with a teacher's behavior that they feel they must report the teacher to the supervisor. Literacy coaches often try to distance themselves from the supervisory act by making the report to a trusted supervisor and asking the supervisor to keep the coach out of the matter. Unfortunately, teachers frequently can make the connection and see how their interactions with a literacy coach led to the supervisor's involvement. The following are a few strategies that you can use to tread these dangerous waters:

- Invite the supervisor to routinely discuss the work teachers are doing with you, the literacy coach, when the supervisor has meetings with teachers. In this way, the supervisor knows what is going on without your needing to report it.

- Encourage the supervisor to ask teachers to select something related to work they're doing with you for him or her to observe when visiting their classrooms. Again, this takes you out of the loop but keeps the supervisor involved with the effort.

- If a team meeting is continually plagued by the negative influence of one member, invite the supervisor to attend the meetings and then provide feedback to the group about how it can function better. Such observations will give the supervisor information to subsequently reflect on in a supervisory meeting with the teacher who is providing the negative effect.

In all these instances, your goal as the literacy coach is to involve the supervisor directly, instead of serving as a go-between for the supervisor and the teachers.

The other instances in which literacy coaches get pulled into the supervision process are those initiated by supervisors. Often, especially when supervisors are unsure or afraid to act, they will ask literacy coaches to perform supervisory duties with underperforming or difficult teachers. Because the best supervision models are formative—that is, they promote teachers' development, rather than merely judge—the line between coaching and supervision is sometimes blurred. A literacy coach can spot the moment he or she crosses the line into supervision by noticing whether his or her interaction with a teacher has any direct bearing on the teacher's performance review. Note that I use the word *direct*. Of course, an effective literacy coach will help teachers improve their practices, and that will lead to stronger performance reviews, but this is not a direct effect. A direct effect would mean that a teacher *must* change as a result of coaching or else face consequences, or that a literacy coach *must* point out certain failings in a teacher because the supervisor does not want to tell the teacher him- or herself.

A clearly written job description is an excellent tool for literacy coaches in these tough situations. So, too, is a strong supervisor for every coach, someone who will talk to the teachers' supervisor when conflicts of interest occur. Finally, some of these problems can be avoided by a frank talk between a literacy coach and teacher supervisor at the outset of their work together. If the teachers' supervisor understands the role of the literacy coach and the model of effective coaching, the supervisor will be less likely to bring the literacy coach into a difficult supervisory matter.

Judge

It's difficult to get close to a teacher's work and not judge it. It's especially difficult given that most literacy coaches are experienced teachers with strong beliefs and values about the work of teaching. However, judging impedes a literacy coach's effectiveness. Clearly, a teacher who feels judged will be less likely to work with a literacy coach and will be vigilant and perhaps reticent when they do work together.

Halting one's judgments is a difficult task. I haven't accomplished it to the extent I'd like to, but I have gotten as far as I have by learning to be present in the moment at hand. If I'm working with a teacher and can be totally engaged with what is going on at that moment, I'm much less likely to slip into judging. I think this is because fear is often attached to judgment. I sometimes feel a need to judge a teacher good or bad, judge a practice successful or unsuccessful, or judge a classroom pleasant or unpleasant because I fear that if I don't, I might let something slip by. In other words, if I haven't judged, then I won't be able to catch what's bad and fix it, and I myself will then be judged a bad coach. There's a cycle of fear being enacted. Of course, this entire notion of catching the bad and fixing it is contrary to the model of coaching presented in this book. That's one of the reasons I strive to be present and to avoid getting caught up in fear and in my need to judge.

Another trap we so easily fall into is the belief that others cannot tell when we are judging them. Part of the reason we have this belief is that it is actually true about half the time. But for every person who is ignorant of our judgment, there is another person who has caught on to it, and people in the latter group are usually those who are closer to us. No matter what we say, our judgments reveal themselves in subtle ways, especially through body language and tone of voice. So, if you are a literacy coach who decides to hide your judgment rather than eliminate it, know that you'll be successful some of the time but not all the time.

Observe Teaching

It surprises many literacy coaches and teachers when I suggest that coaching should not be about the observation of teachers as they teach. Part of this surprise is due to the fact that a peer-coaching model that was popular in the 1980s and early 1990s emphasized just such observation of teaching.

In that model, teachers paired up and used an approach to peer coaching that paralleled the supervisory model that was popular at that time, that is, they had a preobservation conference, the observation, and a postobservation conference. In other words, teachers behaved like supervisors to each other, except for the fact that they did not have control over one another's evaluations or conditions of employment. The centerpiece of this model was the observation of teaching by the person serving as the coach (although both members of the dyad performed each role reciprocally). This model leads teachers to assume that literacy coaches will observe them teaching, and, in fact, many literacy coaches are puzzled about how they could possibly do their jobs if they didn't observe teachers teaching.

The problem with coach-as-observer-of-teaching is that it puts the literacy coach in the position of judge (see the previous discussion of judging in this chapter). In addition, it makes clear that there is a power differential between the teacher and literacy coach. The literacy coach, with his or her ability to observe and judge the teacher, is definitely more powerful. Finally, this approach demonstrates mistrust of the teacher, implying that the teacher's own reporting of what goes on in his or her classroom cannot be trusted.

Now, some teachers tell me that they actually request that a literacy coach observe them because they have a trusting relationship with the literacy coach and really want feedback on what is happening in their classroom. If a teacher really wants the literacy coach to observe, I would never say that my opinion should supersede the teacher's desire. However, I'd also encourage the teacher and coach to think about whether this observation relationship is really necessary and whether it truly does not influence their work together.

My beliefs about this matter are informed by the thinking of Joyce and Showers. These researchers have done the most influential work on coaching in education. Many of their studies were done in the 1980s and 1990s, but their work continues today and their influence remains strong. In the mid-1990s, Joyce and Showers reported their conclusion that if the observation of teaching is occurring in a coach–teacher relationship, the coach should always be the one teaching and the teacher the one observing. They saw benefit to this demonstration teaching, but they did not see that the benefit of the reverse—the coach observing the teacher—was worth the cost to the relationship between teacher and coach (Showers & Joyce, 1996).

Serve as the Expert

Although this topic was discussed in previous chapters, let me remind readers that literacy coaches who behave as experts undo the coaching model.

You can't coach someone if they think you have all the answers; you will end up tutoring them instead. Moreover, when you act as the expert, you convey the sense that there are easy and clearly identified answers to the difficult issues with which teachers struggle. This is inaccurate in some cases and disrespectful of teachers' own knowledge and efforts in all cases. Finally, the literacy coach who is an expert will sooner or later come upon a topic about which he or she is not an expert, and that will lead to an uncomfortable, although perhaps ultimately productive, need to divulge his or her lack of expertise.

Provide Pull-Out Services

Literacy coaches often are asked to work with individual students or groups of students on a regular basis. This work can be valuable to the school, especially if class sizes are large or there is a shortage of expertise in working with readers and writers. However, this is not coaching work. If you do such work, make sure your supervisor and others understand that it takes you away from coaching. This may be the best use of your time—perhaps you'll coach half the time and work with students the other half—so I'm not saying you shouldn't do it. My point is that no one should think that that work is coaching.

On the other hand, literacy coaches sometimes work in classrooms with small groups, often in a guided reading arrangement, in a manner that includes a combination of instructional services and coaching. Here's an example:

●●●●●

Larry is a literacy coach in an elementary school. The third- and fourth-grade teachers recently have begun implementing a reading workshop approach and have asked Larry to spend one hour per day working with guided reading groups. There are two classrooms at each grade level, so Larry spends Mondays and Wednesdays in the third grade, providing 30 minutes of guided reading in each classroom, and does the same for the fourth-grade classes on Tuesdays and Thursdays. Larry recognizes that his role during much of this time is a provider of instruction, not a literacy coach. However, he also knows that this work furthers his literacy coaching duties in several ways. First, on occasion the classroom teacher sits in on his guided reading lesson, when she is not working with a guided reading group herself. Also, Larry has conferences with the classroom teacher on a regular basis about what the teachers are doing in their guided reading groups, the progress they observe the children making, and the makeup of the groups. These conversations enable Larry and the teacher to discuss ideas about ongoing assessment and to share ideas for strategy instruction. In addition, Larry is consistently the one who suggests moving children among guided reading groups to better meet their instructional needs; he is fairly certain that without his demonstration and reminders, the teachers would not move the children. In these ways, then, coaching enters into the work Larry does while providing in-classroom instruction.

Literacy coaches often have a difficult time saying no to requests to work with children. This may be in part because they love working with students, and because they hate to turn down any requests. However, it also could be because they are not adequately focused on their goals. If you as a literacy coach are asked to work with students, reflect on how such work would or wouldn't help you to further your coaching goals, and then act accordingly.

It is no coincidence that the final section of the conclusion addresses tasks that literacy coaches should not do. I repeatedly encounter literacy coaches who are doing just such tasks—supervising, judging, serving as the expert, observing teachers, or providing pull-out services—and don't know how to get out of them. My goal in ending with this information is to provide a final reminder to literacy coaches that they must be clear about what their jobs entail and then stick to those tasks whenever possible. Think of the tasks that literacy coaches don't do as bearing a road sign that says, "Danger: Proceed with Caution." Many literacy coaches certainly survive even when they do such tasks, but the risk of resulting problems is great. If possible, it is best to avoid these tasks altogether.

Conclusion

The lists above are not definitive. Literacy coaches perform many duties that are not on either list. My purpose in mentioning the items in this chapter is to remind literacy coaches about the general thrust of their work. They are on the job to provide support, encouragement, and responsiveness to teachers. They are not there to do the principal's job or the teacher's job, and they are not there to make others impressed or uncomfortable.

Literacy coaching is exhilarating when it goes well. It's exciting to work alongside another professional to help students achieve. When literacy coaching doesn't go well, the temptation is to feel like a failure. Instead, I would encourage you to enjoy the challenge and realize that coaching, like teaching, is about problem finding and problem solving. Literacy coaching is best when you approach it as your best self—someone who is kind, centered, open, and trustworthy. If you live your literacy coaching life with the belief that coaching is at heart about relationships and growth, not answers and authority, you will be a genuine literacy coach who is successful in supporting teachers. I hope you enjoy literacy coaching as much as I do.

RESOURCES FOR LITERACY COACHES

Every chapter in this book closes with suggested resources related to the ideas in that chapter. Here, I want to suggest a different kind of resource: yourself. Keep a log of your initiatives, thoughts, insights, questions, notes, and anything else that will serve as a record of your literacy coaching work. You might want to put the log in an accordion file with sections. Then, when you are seeking sources for assistance, you can include your log as a resource for information and solutions. Certainly, you want to benefit from others' work, but as your coach, I want to remind you of all that you know and encourage you to trust yourself as well as others.

As your text-based coach, I'm interested in hearing what you think. Coaching is without a doubt a reciprocal act, and I would like to learn from you about what you find helpful in the book and what you find unhelpful. My e-mail address is toll@insightbb.com. Please contact me with your comments.

Key Questions Answered in This Book Listed by Topic

Note: Some questions are cross-referenced under more than one topic.

Coaches' Duties

Coaching Groups

Coaching Individuals

Communication

Difficult Situations

The Effects of Literacy Coaching

Educational Change

General Information About Literacy Coaches

Information About This Book

Organizing Yourself and Your Work

Resistant Teachers

Starting Out

Survival on the Job

Working With a Variety of Teachers

Working With Principals

APPENDIX B

A Narrative Bibliography: Where Do These Ideas Come From?

This is not a typical bibliography, as you already can see. It isn't a mere list of books and articles to which you can turn to read more. Rather, this appendix provides information about the resources cited throughout the book. But even then, it's not your typical annotated bibliography. I hope instead to weave a brief narrative about significant ideas presented in each chapter. What I wish to do is extend our discussions from the previous chapters into this appendix, chatting one more time about topics related to literacy coaching. My comments and the references I cite refer to specific sections or statements I make in a given chapter to which I'll direct your attention. Topics are organized by the order in which they appear in the chapters.

Introduction: What Is This Book About? Who Is It For?

What Is Literacy Coaching?

The International Reading Association has produced a position statement, *The Role and Qualifications of the Reading Coach in the United States*, which provides a useful resource for those trying to identify the duties of a literacy coach and for those wishing to ensure that literacy coaches have the needed knowledge, background, and experiences. This position statement can be accessed at www.reading.org/positions/1065.html

Coaching Affects School Culture

Although research has not been done to show the direct influence of coaching on school culture, there is a great deal of research on how school culture can be changed or at least influenced. If you are interested in reading more about this, you might look at the works of Sarason (Sarason, 1996; Sarason & Lorentz, 1998) and Deal (Deal & Peterson, 1999). In addition,

DiPardo (1997) is among the scholars who have examined the effect of collaboration on school cultures. She finds that school cultures can inhibit collaboration in many instances, but in the best of cases the opposite happens and collaboration and school culture work symbiotically to promote risk-taking, interdependence, and positive change. Little (1990) has examined teacher collaboration, including models that use coaching, and suggests that those collaborations which produce joint work—that is, work that is dependent on the collaboration in order to be successful—are significant in changing teachers' work and the work environment.

Significant Change in Education

The limited effects of many change efforts in education have been well documented by Tyack and Cuban (1995) as well as Gibboney (1994). These authors demonstrate that educational changes attempted throughout the 20th century had limited lasting effect, if any at all. Sarason (1996) argues that significant educational change will only take place when school cultures change. One of the consequences of arguments such as his has been the implementation of shared decision making. Anderson (1998) critiques shared decision making, demonstrating its many limitations, yet also provides suggestions for how collaborations can be meaningful and significant in supporting educational change.

The Importance of Reflection in Teaching

I find the most helpful works on teacher reflection to be written by Zeichner and Liston (1996) and Schön (1987). These works give thorough overviews of what reflection in teaching looks like and how it can be fostered. In the domain of professional development, Richardson (in Ross & Regan, 1993) has suggested that a constructivist approach that emphasizes learner control and professional interaction (such as that found in a coaching model) leads to greater teacher reflection than professional development that focuses on conveying knowledge to teachers (such as a traditional workshop approach). In addition, Harste and Burke (1977) have reported that all teaching is influenced by teachers' theoretical belief systems, although not all teachers can state their beliefs explicitly. Coaching can assist with this kind of deep reflection.

Characteristics of Adult Learners

For more on characteristics of adult learners, go to either LInC Online's Staff Development—Adult Characteristics webpage at www-ed.fnal.gov/lincon/staff_adult.shtml or read "30 Things We Know for Sure About Adult

Learning" at http://honolulu.hawaii.edu/intranet/committees/FacDevCom/guidebk/teachtip/adults-3.htm.

Related to the research on adult learners is the research on the construction of meaning. Educators increasingly theorize that learning is a process of creating understanding through an active constructive process, and that this learning is best done—or, from some theorists' perspectives, only done—in social contexts in which the environment contributes to that construction. To read more on these ideas, look at the work of Fosnot (1996) on constructivism in general or a book edited by Phillips (2000) for varied perspectives and critiques on constructivism.

Reading First

You can learn more about Reading First from the website developed by the Reading First Subgrant Technical Assistance center at the North Central Regional Education Laboratory (www.ncrel.org/rf/).

Head Start

The literacy coaching initiative for Head Start is part of the Strategic Teacher Education Program (STEP) component of the grant reauthorization of 2003. More information can be found at www.headstartinfo.org or www.hsnrc.org/STEP1102/mcworkbook.pdf.

The Conventional Wisdom That Schools Are Broken

The most recent wave of school reform began with *A Nation at Risk: The Imperative for Educational Reform* (National Commission on Excellence in Education, 1983), a report issued by the U.S. government that stated that schools were in crisis. This report was followed by a series of reform efforts designed to alter the perceived state of public school in the United States. A review of what has happened in the name of reform over the last 20 years can be found in *A Nation Reformed? American Education 20 Years After* A Nation at Risk (Gordon, 2003). In addition, challenges to the assumption that education has been in crisis can be found in *The Manufactured Crisis: Myths, Fraud, and the Attack on America's Public Schools* (Berliner & Biddle, 1995) and in much of the work by Bracey, including his annual reports on the status of education in the October issues of *Phi Delta Kappan* and his books *Setting the Record Straight: Responses to Misconceptions About Public Education in the United States* (1997) and *What You Should Know About the War Against America's Public Schools* (2003).

Social and Political Lenses on Education

You can read about the political nature of education in Spring's book *Political Agendas for Education: From the Religious Right to the Green Party* (2002). I found this book extremely helpful in enabling me to sort out the various forces that influence education, especially foundations and private-sector organizations. For more on political aspects of literacy education, read Shannon's book *Reading Poverty* (1998).

Chapter 1: What Do the Experts Say About Educational Change?

Technologies of Change

My discussion of the technologies of change comes from extensive reading of the educational change literature. Below is a list of sources in which you can read more about each of the proposed technologies.

Change Leadership

● Create and lead learning communities (Barth, 1990)

● Develop the culture of the school (Peterson, 1988)

● Develop a vision for the school (Schlechty, 1990)

● Have a moral orientation, focusing on values and trust (Sergiovanni, 1992)

● Serve as strategic thinkers (Hallinger & McCary, 1990)

Change Implementers

● Determine how to meet school district goals (Sizer, 1992)

● Focus on philosophy prior to activities (Au & Scheu, 1996)

● Interact and communicate (Tye & Tye, 1984)

● Understand how their beliefs and practices derive from their experiences and the influence of their culture (Briscoe, 1994)

● View themselves as learners in a community of learners (Hendricks-Lee, Soled, & Yinger, 1995)

The Innovation Itself

● Constructivist thinking (Fosnot, 1986)

● Dimensions of learning (Marzano, 1992)

● Hands-on math (National Council of Teachers of Mathematics, 1989)

● Liberatory pedagogy (Levine, Lowe, Peterson, & Tenorio, 1995)

● Literature-based reading (Routman, 1994)

- Multiple intelligences (Gardner, 1983)
- Portfolio assessment (Perrone, 1991)
- Students as knowledge workers (Schlechty, 1990)
- Values education (Bennett, 1993)

The Process

- Alter cultures (Sweeney & Harris, 2002)
- Change behaviors through mastery learning (Stallings, 1981)
- Change learning processes through inquiry (Stokes, 2001)
- Change thinking (Costa & Garmston, 2002)
- Develop a systems perspective (Elmore, 1978)

What Are You Trying to Change?

Range of Change and/or Mismatch Among Foci of Change. Le Fevre and Richardson (2002) conducted a study of teacher leaders who had coaching roles that involved leading the implementation of various early literacy programs. The researchers learned that these literacy coaches perceived a range of duties for which they were responsible. Some saw themselves as advocates for students or teachers, others saw themselves as visionaries, and still others saw themselves as monitors of quality assurance in the program implementation. These are just three of the considerable number of competing roles that Le Fevre and Richardson identified. Along with competing understandings of their roles, these teacher leaders differed in their understanding of what, if anything, they needed to change.

Change Focused on Behavior. A book that provides an enthusiastic depiction of communication tools and attitudes for improving behaviors is *Whale Done! The Power of Positive Relationships* by Blanchard (2002). Glasser's book, *The Quality School: Managing Students Without Coercion* (1992), applies his Choice Theory to education. Choice Theory is based on the notion that genes drive our behavior, and our behavior focuses on moving from less pleasurable to more pleasurable situations. We choose our behavior, but our choices are dictated by this goal of experiencing more pleasure. When applied to coaching, Choice Theory would suggest that a coach should influence teachers' behaviors by making it pleasurable for the teachers to do what the coach wants.

A criticism of behavior-focused approaches to change, whether in schools, places of employment, homes, or society in general, is provided by Kohn in *Punished by Rewards: The Trouble With Gold Stars, Incentive Plans,*

A's, Praise and Other Bribes (1999). Kohn cites numerous studies that demonstrate that behavior-focused approaches to change do not create lasting effects. An additional critique of change focused on behavior, in this case aimed directly at coaches, is in Flaherty's *Coaching: Evoking Excellence in Others* (1999).

Change Focused on Attitude. A great deal of information about the Concerns-Based Adoption Model (CBAM) (Hord, 1987) can be found online at the National Staff Development Council's webpage (www.nsdc.org, search "CBAM"), the National Academy of Sciences' webpage (www.nas.edu/rise/backg4a.htm), and the Southwest Educational Development Laboratory's webpage (www.sedl.org/pubs/catalog/items/cbam.html).

Change Focused on Cognition. The leading resource on coaching to change thinking is the work of Costa and his colleagues at the Center for Cognitive Coaching. This work can be accessed through the center's website at www.cognitivecoaching.com or through the book *Cognitive Coaching: A Foundation for Renaissance Schools* by Costa and Garmston (2002).

Change Focused on Inquiry. *The Art of Classroom Inquiry: A Handbook for Teacher-Researchers* by Hubbard and Power (1993) provides an overview of approaches for teacher inquiry. A great resource for understanding one school's inquiry process, which led to substantial changes in spelling instruction, is *Spelling Inquiry: How One Elementary School Caught the Mnemonic Plague* (Chandler, 1999). Another resource comes from the National Council of Teachers of English (NCTE) Reading Initiative (2000), which uses an inquiry approach in parts of its professional development program. An explanation of the Reading Initiative's perspective on change can be found online in its handbook at www.ncte.org/library/files/Profdev/onsite/RI/ResearchBase.PDF.

Change Focused on Systems. An excellent resource is Black's (2002) book, *Get Over It! Education Reform Is Dead, Now What?*, which encourages an open systems approach—encouraging systems themselves to change. Another book is *A Simpler Way* by Wheatley and Kellner-Rogers (1996), which discusses self-organization in systems—an approach in which individuals recognize their contributions to systems and develop skills for organizing themselves and, subsequently, the systems.

Change Focused on Culture. Hargreaves (1994) raises questions about school cultures in his book *Changing Teachers, Changing Times: Teachers' Word and Culture in the Postmodern Age*. Schlechty (1992) provides a new vision of school culture in *Creating Schools for the 21st Century: Practical Guidelines for Achieving Systemwide Change on a Day-to-Day Basis.*

Chapter 2: Why Is Change So Difficult?

Buddhist Concepts of Change

If you are interested in reading more about Buddhist concepts of change, you might want to read selections of *Nothing Special: Living Zen* (Beck, 1993), which provides transcripts of dharma (wisdom) teachings by a Zen teacher, or Epstein's *Going to Pieces Without Falling Apart: A Buddhist Perspective on Wholeness* (1998). The latter is especially written for someone who is not a serious Buddhist practitioner. I also have a chapter in a forthcoming book called *Spirituality, Action, and Pedagogy: Teaching From the Heart* (Ashton & Denton, in press) that will address additional insights on change that I have drawn from Buddhist teachings.

Teacher Action Research

Teacher action research often is taught as a discrete research process, a kind of applied research that is often done by practitioners who are pursuing graduate degrees. However, teaching at its best is a kind of ongoing action research. A book that I find useful in giving examples of how teachers' action research has affected their teaching lives is *Inside/Outside: Teacher Research and Knowledge* (Cochran-Smith & Lytle, 1993).

Literacy Centers and Reading Workshop

A book that gives a good description of how to use reading centers while conducting guided reading is *Guided Reading: Good First Teaching for All Children* (Fountas & Pinnell, 1996). A book that gives a description of how to have children do reading and journaling while you conduct guided reading is *On Solid Ground: Strategies for Teaching Reading K–3* (Taberski, 2000).

Problems With Demanding Change

Eaton and Johnson (2001) discuss the advantages of either a "pull" or "push" approach to coaching. The "pull" approach is one that is more demanding and places the coach in a supervisory role. Little (1990) analyzes teachers' responses to coaching and collaboration and notes that teachers frequently feel that asking for or needing help is a sign of inferiority. Little stresses that collaboration, including coaching, is most effective when it occurs in a situation of interdependence among all participants.

Traumatic Change

Fournies (2000) includes in his book on coaching a discussion of the negative effects of traumatic change, which he refers to as *punishment*. Fournies points out that this tactic for promoting change leads to the side effects of apprehension and aggression.

Finding Time to Talk

The issue of time is a difficult one. Hargreaves (1994) has written extensively about the intensification of teachers' work (i.e., the increased demands placed upon teachers) and the perception that more time is the solution. He sees the need for teachers to have more planning time, but he cautions that such time will not solve all problems created by the intensification of teachers' work. Also, he recognizes that such planning time may be used up by counterproductive "contrived collegiality" (p. 195) (i.e., mandated collaboration). DiPardo (1997) notes that perceptions of what is "enough" time for collaboration vary by the nature of the work and the effectiveness teachers feel. When teachers' collaborative work will truly make a difference, issues of time become less significant.

Chapter 3: How Do I Begin My Work as a Literacy Coach?

First Impressions

The book *Reading People: How to Understand People and Predict Their Behavior—Anytime, Anyplace* by Dimitrius and Mazzarella (1999) includes a chapter on first impressions. It is written from the perspective of how first impressions can help one to understand others, but in the process the authors demonstrate that first impressions do make a difference in how one is perceived. Another useful resource is *Reading Faces: Window to the Soul?* (Zebrowitz, 1997).

Including Parents

Many resources provide suggestions for including parents in efforts to increase students' literacy achievement. These resources provide a range of perspectives on the role of parents and the relationships between parents and school personnel. Epstein (2001) has helped me to consider that range of perspectives and understand the implications of various approaches to parents and parent involvement. Ideas for making good first impressions at open houses can be found at www.naesp.org/ContentLoad.do?contentId=273.

Chapter 4: What Are the Qualities of an Effective Literacy Coach?

National Reading Panel Report

The National Reading Panel Report and a summary of the report can be found online at www.nationalreadingpanel.org. Although the report itself is much longer than the summary report (over 600 pages, compared to 32 pages), I encourage you to familiarize yourself with the entire report. Many readers of the two documents find that they present different angles on the same information.

A critique of what the report does—and doesn't—say is in Garan's book *Resisting Reading Mandates: How to Triumph With the Truth* (2002). Tim Shanahan, a member of the National Reading Panel, responds to critiques by Garan and others in "Research-Based Reading Instruction: Myths About the National Reading Panel Report" (2003).

Expertise

Evans (1999) provides a thoughtful reflection on the struggle she had with the concept of expertise. As a university professor, she engaged in a collaborative partnership with a classroom teacher in which she wanted to be equals. Despite these intentions, she found herself with greater power than the classroom teacher and eventually resolved that that positioning might actually be most beneficial to their relationship. Evans's work contradicts my belief that literacy coaches should not act as experts. In fact, she makes evident in her article that her findings contradict what she generally believes. Please note that her study involved a university professor and a classroom teacher, not a literacy coach and a classroom teacher. I refer to this article here because it presents a thoughtful reflection on the role of power (of which expertise is a kind) in collaborative relationships.

Noting Others' Mistakes

The concept of collecting "the goods" on other people is discussed in Berne's book *Games People Play: The Psychology of Human Relationships* (1973). In the 1970s the field of transactional analysis provided a popular way for many of us to consider how we interacted with other people, and Berne took the concepts of transactional analysis a step further by describing human interactions as games of a sort.

Respect

An intriguing analysis of many aspects of respect is Lawrence-Lightfoot's *Respect: An Exploration* (1999).

Chapter 5: How Can I Communicate Well With Teachers?

Listening

Did you know that there is an International Listening Association? Visit www.listen.org for more information, including a list of 10 irritating listening habits. This list won't surprise you—it includes such annoying habits as rushing the speaker and trying to stop the speaker's story with your own—but it serves as a good reminder, which we all need occasionally.

Another excellent resource on listening is *The Lost Art of Listening: How Learning to Listen Can Improve Relationships* by Nichols (1995). If you are like me, you may think, I've known how to listen since I was born; reading a book on listening would be like reading a book on breathing. First, remember that listening is different from hearing. Second, this book on listening is really a book on being the kind of person who makes connections with others. One of the author's insights that I found most helpful is that listening is really about suspending one's own needs. This is important for a literacy coach to remember, because a literacy coach who is "listening" merely for an opportunity to interject his or her beliefs about what a teacher should be doing is not listening at all.

A third resource is chapter 6 of *Reading People* by Dimitrius and Mazzarella (1999). This chapter provides a review of listening and questioning strategies. Two tips that I find particularly helpful are (1) to disclose a bit about yourself when another person is disclosing information about him- or herself and (2) to consider the context when another person tells you about a problem, so you can recognize if the problem reflects the person's environment or if it is more chronic.

Communication Strategies

The work of Deborah Tannen has influenced the thinking of many people regarding how humans communicate. Tannen is probably most well known for her work on communication differences between men and women, but I have gotten a great deal of insight from her work on communication styles more generally. *Talking From 9 to 5: How Women's and Men's Conversational Styles Affect Who Gets Heard, Who Gets Credit, and What Gets Done at Work*

(1994) and *That's Not What I Meant! How Conversational Style Makes or Breaks Relationships* (1986) will be of particular interest to literacy coaches. Also, if you are working in a region where you did not grow up or are working with people from all over the United States or the world, you may want to check out chapter 3 of *That's Not What I Meant!* because it details some differences in communication style that are geographically based.

Chapter 6: How Do I Coach Individuals?

Teaching as an Individual Act

Little (1990) provides insight regarding the nature of the teacher's solitary work in her analysis of just the opposite, teacher collaboration. Among her points are the influence of school cultures on teacher isolation or collaboration and the insight that "independent trial and error serves as the principal route to competence" (p. 515) for teachers. Little suggests that some activities of groups of teachers that look like collaboration actually reinforce teachers' isolation and independence from each other. This occurs because such "collaborations" actually are rooted in discourses of the immediate, context-driven, and unique nature of the teacher's problems and knowledge.

Kinds of Data

An excellent source of ideas for kinds of data that might be collected about students' literate behaviors and processes is *Windows Into Literacy: Assessing Learners K–8* (Rhodes & Shanklin, 1993). Among the many tools that are unique to this resource is the Survey of Displayed Literacy Stimuli (pp. 92–94), which provides guidelines for doing an environmental scan of one's classroom in order to look at the classroom from the perspective of a student and note how literacy is represented in that classroom.

Chapter 7: How Do I Coach Teacher Teams and Study Groups?

Goal Setting

Eaton and Johnson (2001) provide an acronym for gauging the quality of goals. Goals should be SMART: Specific, Measured, Achievable, Relevant, and Timed (p. 31). With this acronym, the authors offer a tool for gauging the usefulness of a goal. Literacy coaches might review each of the terms as they work with teachers to develop goals. In other words, literacy coaches might share the acronym and ask teachers if they'd like to use it to evaluate the quality of a proposed goal. I'd suggest letting teachers take the lead in evaluating their goals at each step, so they are not intimidated by the coach taking the lead in determining whether a goal is specific, measured, achievable, relevant, or timed.

Facilitating Team Work

In *Difficult Conversations: How to Discuss What Matters Most* (1999), Stone, Patton, and Heen include a useful chapter on problem solving. This chapter will enable you as a coach to see how you can be a leader in solving problems, rather than a victim of problems. It might be a good chapter to share with the entire team with whom you are working. Another excellent resource is Achinstein's book, *Community, Diversity, and Conflict Among Schoolteachers: The Ties That Blind* (2002). Achinstein examines collaboration in two school settings and draws some useful insights; for instance, she suggests that collaboration leads as much to anxiety as productivity, but that conflict may actually lead to healthier schools because it pushes staff members to think beyond their familiar comfort zones.

Difficulties in Collaborating and Communicating

A number of authors have written about the pitfalls of collaborative efforts. Specific to the topic of coaching, Corrie (1995) found that when the "rules" of staff collaboration were unclear, the collaboration was unsuccessful and led to pseudocollaboration. Hargreaves suggests that a great deal of "contrived collegiality" exists in schools today (1994, p. 195). He uses this term to describe the kinds of collaborations that look good on the surface but really involve little authentic interaction among participants. Instead of authentic interaction, contrived collegiality is "going along to get along." Participants are usually told they must work together and are told what the outcome must be, and then the "collaborators" play-act the process in order to look like good workers. Little (1987) has written about her similar concerns that collaboration is not as collaborative as it might seem. Another critique of collaboration comes from Anderson (1998), who suggests that most models of school staff collaboration and decision making actually manipulate staff members into maintaining the status quo. In other words, collaboration is used as a kind of rubber stamp to get staff members to agree with what already has been decided.

On the other hand, Meyer (1998) suggests that collaborative teams can be difficult because they do exactly what they are supposed to do—disrupt the status quo. In the process, he says, teachers and others become uncomfortable and need to negotiate the difficulties of finding new ways to do their work and to work together.

Difficult Conversations

Difficult Conversations: How to Discuss What Matters Most (Stone, Patton, & Heen, 1999), referred to previously in this narrative bibliography, is an excellent book for sorting through the struggles that all groups have when they attempt to form teams. I know that some schools have used this book as a focus of staffwide discussion and reflection. This seems like an excellent idea to me because the suggestions in the book will be most effective when more than one person knows and uses them. The book *Connect: 12 Vital Ties That Open Your Heart, Lengthen Your Life, and Deepen Your Soul* (Hallowell, 1999) also has suggestions for getting through difficult conversations.

What the Research Says

If you are striving to be an informed consumer of research, you may enjoy Bracey's book *Bail Me Out! Handling Difficult Data and Tough Questions About Public Schools* (2000). A concise overview of how to manage educational research is in an article by Carnahan and Fitzpatrick (2003), and a thought-provoking book about the complexity of various "knowledges" found in education is Carr and Kemmis's *Becoming Critical: Education, Knowledge, and Action Research* (1986).

Dysfunctional Groups

The book *Hot Buttons: How to Resolve Conflict and Cool Everyone Down* (Evans & Cohen, 2000) is like a master course on addressing conflict in groups. In fact, the lead author of the book calls herself a "Conflict Coach." Using the techniques in this book may help you determine whether the group you are working with is hopelessly dysfunctional: If the techniques work at all, then the group may be able to function successfully, albeit with a little effort. Coaches dealing with dysfunctional groups also may find help in McClain and Romaine's *The Everything Managing People Book: Quick and Easy Ways to Build, Motivate, and Nurture a First-Rate Team* (2002), which includes a chapter on addressing work group dynamics.

Discussions in Response to What Was Read

There are a great many ideas in professional literature for teachers about how to get students to respond authentically to what they've read, most of which facilitate discussion. Although teachers in a study group do not have the same qualities as children in, say, a literature circle, there are parallels, and many of the same strategies that work for students can be adapted for teacher study groups. I like the "Tell Me" strategy (Chambers, 1995) in which the facilitator encourages participants to tell him or her something, which is different from asking participants to answer "my" questions. There are four "tell me" prompts: (1) Tell me what you liked, (2) tell me what you didn't like, (3) tell me what you found puzzling, and (4) tell me what connections you made.

Chapter 8: How Do I Deal With Difficult Teachers?

Working Across Differences

Ellsworth (1997) has one of the most thought-provoking perspectives on efforts to communicate and collaborate. Her background in film studies, combined with research from psychoanalysis, gives educators some unique perspectives on teaching and what often is called communicative dialogue. She argues that such dialogue is never going to be completely successful, given the complexity of the communication act and the positioning of those participating. However, she urges educators to work difference, which involves recognizing that differences exist among collaborators, expecting and planning for conflict, acknowledging that there will be a struggle and that complete understanding will not take place, and doing the work anyway (Ellsworth, 1997; Ellsworth & Miller, 1996). Ellsworth suggests that, rather than trying to eliminate conflict in collaboration, we should make it visible and include it as part of the work.

And, *Not* Or

Stone, Patton, and Heen, in their powerful book *Difficult Conversations* (1999), suggest that participants in a difficult conversation break away from who's right and who's wrong and focus instead on the stories each party has to tell. This is a useful step toward "and" rather than "or."

Resistance in Organizations

de Dreu and de Vries (1997) have done some fascinating work on the role of dissenters in organizations. They have found that dissenters can help groups to produce better work if they get group members to think differently about the topic at hand. However, they have also found that dissenters aren't automatically successful in creating such alternate or expanded views of the topic. The success of dissenters depends on a number of factors. Dissent will be most effective when dissent is encouraged in the group, when the dissenter is confident and is respected by others on the team (either because of their talent, because they have more power, or because they are part of an "in" group), and when the topic is of high importance to participants.

Chapter 9: What About *This* Issue?

Raising Test Scores

For more information about curriculum mapping and aligning the enacted, written, and tested curriculum, see the Learning Point Associates' website at www.learningpt.org.

Mirroring

Boreen (2000) provides additional information about mirroring in *Mentoring Beginning Teachers: Guiding, Reflecting, Coaching.*

Professional Development Workshops

Lyons and Pinnell (2001) provide a great deal of information about planning and implementing a program of professional development in their book *Systems for Change in Literacy Education: A Guide to Professional Development.* See also Sweeney's (2003) practical and readable book *Learning Along the Way: Professional Development By and For Teachers.* I like this book because it helps literacy coaches think about how to respond to their particular setting.

Student Assessment

Although it is not directed specifically at coaches, the book *Interactive Assessment: Teachers, Parents, and Students as Partners* (2003) by Tierney, Crumpler, Bertelsen, and Bond provides practical ideas for thinking about a schoolwide assessment program and shared roles in implementing it. This will be a valuable resource for coaches who are involved in any aspect of student assessment practices.

Chapter 10: How Do I Survive This Job?

Stress Management

In his book, *Connect*, Hallowell (1999) provides a document that he originally prepared for the Department of Chemistry at Harvard University.

This document gives an overview of issues related to stress and how to address them.

A problem I constantly face is in taking on too many responsibilities in my personal and professional lives and then feeling overwhelmed. The book *Beyond Juggling: Rebalancing Your Busy Life* (Sandholtz, 2002) provided insight for me about how other professionals have achieved balance in their lives.

Conclusion: What Do Coaches Do? What Don't They Do?

Locating Resources

Among the many websites that can provide resources for literacy coaches are the following:

- Alliance for Excellent Education: www.all4ed.org
- International Reading Association: www.reading.org
- Learning Point Associates (including the Literacy Center at the North Central Regional Educational Laboratory): www.learningpt.org
- National Council of Teachers of English: www.ncte.org
- National Institute for Literacy: www.nifl.gov
- National Staff Development Council: www.nsdc.org
- Pacific Resources for Education and Learning: www.prel.org

Teacher Observation

If you absolutely must do observations of teachers in their classrooms, because of a mandate that you can't get around, then you might want to read Lyons' chapter in *Learning from Teaching in Literacy Education* (Rodgers & Pinnell, 2002). She gives a step-by-step process for what she calls *Analytic Coaching*, a series of steps that a coach and teacher can use to guide the coach's observation and subsequent follow-up meeting with the teacher.

Peer Coaching

For an overview of a traditional model of peer coaching, see "Professional collaboration: Empowering school personnel through peer coaching" (Anderson et al., 1994).

Judging and Fear

Fear often leads to judging. I have thought a lot about the fear we all feel at times as educators, and the detrimental effect it has on our work, since reading Palmer's book *The Courage to Teach: Exploring the Inner Landscape of a Teacher's Life* (1998). I'd encourage you to place this book at the top of your reading list, if you haven't read it already. Palmer's work continues to touch my heart and mind as I learn and grow in this profession.

This narrative bibliography provides sources of key ideas that have helped me to develop my coaching practices. It also provides sources to which you can turn if you'd like to read further about some of the topics I've touched on. You may want to develop your own narrative bibliography in the form of a computer document or series of index cards on which you note important ideas that you get from your reading and the source in which you found them. Narrative bibliographies can be of great use for future reference. I hope this one serves that purpose for you.

REFERENCES

Achinstein, B. (2002). *Community, diversity, and conflict among schoolteachers: The ties that blind*. New York: Teachers College Press.

Anderson, D.M., Vail, C.O., Jones, K., & Huntington, D. (1994, April). *Professional collaboration: Empowering school personnel through peer coaching*. Paper presented at the Annual International Convention of the Council for Exceptional Children, Denver, CO. (ERIC Document Reproduction Service No. ED371496)

Anderson, G.L. (1998). Toward authentic participation: Deconstructing the discourses of participatory reforms in education. *American Educational Research Journal, 35*(4), 571–603.

Ashton, R.W., & Denton, D. (in press). *Spirituality, action, and pedagogy: Teaching from the heart*. New York: Peter Lang.

Au, K.H., & Scheu, J.A. (1996). Journey toward holistic instruction: Supporting teachers' growth. *The Reading Teacher, 49*, 468–477.

Barth, R.S. (1990). *Improving schools from within: Teachers, parents, and principals can make the difference*. San Francisco: Jossey-Bass.

Beck, C.J. (1993). *Nothing special: Living Zen*. San Francisco: Harper.

Bennett, W.J. (Ed). (1993). *The book of virtues: A treasury of great moral stories*. New York: Simon & Schuster.

Berliner, D.C., & Biddle, B.J. (1995). *The manufactured crisis: Myths, fraud, and the attack on America's public schools*. Reading, MA: Addison-Wesley.

Berne, E. (1973). *Games people play: The psychology of human relationships*. New York: Ballantine.

Biklen, S.K. (1995). *School work: Gender and the cultural construction of teaching*. New York: Teachers College Press.

Black, C. (2002). *Get over it! Education reform is dead, now what?* Portsmouth, NH: Heinemann.

Blanchard, K.H. (2002). *Whale done! The power of positive relationships*. New York: Free Press.

Boorstein, S. (1995). *It's easier than you think: The Buddhist way to happiness*. San Francisco: Harper.

Boreen, J. (2000). *Mentoring beginning teachers: Guiding, reflecting, coaching*. Portland, ME: Stenhouse.

Bracey, G.W. (1997). *Setting the record straight: Responses to misconceptions about public education in the United States*. Alexandria, VA: Association for Supervision and Curriculum Development.

Bracey, G.W. (2000). *Bail me out! Handling difficult data and tough questions about public schools*. Thousand Oaks, CA: Corwin Press.

Bracey, G.W. (2003). *What you should know about the war against America's public schools*. Boston: Allyn & Bacon.

Briscoe, C. (1994). Cognitive frameworks and teaching practices: A case study of teacher learning and change. *Journal of Educational Thought, 28*(3), 286–309.

Carnahan, D., & Fitzpatrick, M. (2003). Don't get buried under a mountain of research. *Journal of Staff Development, 24*(2), 18–22.

Carr, W., & Kemmis, S. (1986). *Becoming critical: Education, knowledge, and action research*. London: Falmer.

Chambers, A. (1995). *Tell me: Children, reading, and talk*. York, ME: Stenhouse.

Chandler, K. (1999). *Spelling inquiry: How one elementary school caught the mnemonic plague*. York, MN: Stenhouse.

Cochran-Smith, M., & Lytle, S.L. (Eds.). (1993). *Inside/outside: Teacher research and knowledge*. New York: Teachers College Press.

Corrie, L. (1995). The structure and culture of staff collaboration: Managing meaning and opening doors. *Educational Review, 47*(1), 89–99.

Costa, A.L., & Garmston, R.J. (2002). *Cognitive coaching: A foundation for Renaissance schools* (2nd ed.). Norwood, MA: Christopher-Gordon.

Cuban, L. (1998). How schools change reforms: Redefining reform success and failure. *Teachers College Record, 99*(3), 453–477.

Deal, T.E., & Peterson, K.D. (1999). *Shaping school culture: The heart of leadership*. San Francisco: Jossey-Bass.

de Dreu, C.K.W., & de Vries, N.K. (1997). Minority dissent in organizations. In C.K.W. de Dreu & E. Van de Vliet (Eds.), *Using conflict in organizations* (pp. 72–86). Thousand Oaks, CA: Sage.

Dimitrius, J., & Mazzarella, M. (1999). *Reading people: How to understand people and predict their behavior—anytime, anyplace*. New York: Ballantine.

DiPardo, A. (1997). Of war, doom, and laughter: Images of collaboration in the public-school workplace. *Teacher Education Quarterly, 24*(1), 89–104.

Eaton, J., & Johnson, R. (2000). *Coaching successfully*. London: Dorling Kindersley.

Ellsworth, E.A. (1997). *Teaching positions: Difference, pedagogy, and the power of address*. New York: Teachers College Press.

Ellsworth, E.A., & Miller, J.L. (1996). Working difference in education. *Curriculum Inquiry, 26*(3), 245–263.

Elmore, R. (1978). Organizational models of social program implementation. In D. Mann (Ed.), *Making change happen?* (pp. 185–223). New York: Teachers College Press.

Epstein, J.L. (2001). *School, family, and community partnerships: Your handbook for action* (2nd ed.). Thousand Oaks, CA: Corwin Press.

Epstein, M. (1998). *Going to pieces without falling apart: A Buddhist perspective on wholeness*. New York: Broadway.

Evans, K.S. (1999). Negotiating roles in collaborative literacy research: Re-examining issues of power and equity. *Language Arts, 77*(2), 128–136.

Evans, S., & Cohen, S.S. (2000). *Hot buttons: How to resolve conflict and cool everyone down*. New York: Cliff Street.

Festinger, L. (1957). *A theory of cognitive dissonance*. Evanston, IL: Row, Peterson.

Flaherty, J. (1999). *Coaching: Evoking excellence in others*. Boston: Butterworth-Heinemann.

Fosnot, C.T. (1996). *Constructivism: Theory, perspectives, and practices*. New York: Teachers College Press.

Fountas, I.C., & Pinnell, G.S. (1996). *Guided reading: Good first teaching for all children*. Portsmouth, NH: Heinemann.

Fournies, F.F. (2000). *Coaching for improved work performance* (Rev. ed.). New York: McGraw-Hill.

Fullan, M., & Hargreaves, A. (1996). *What's worth fighting for in your school?* New York: Teachers College Press.

Garan, E.M. (2002). *Resisting reading mandates: How to triumph with the truth*. Portsmouth, NH: Heinemann.

Gardner, H. (1983). *Frames of mind: The theory of multiple intelligences*. New York: Basic Books.

Gibboney, R.A. (1994). *The stone trumpet: A story of practical school reform 1960–1990*. Albany: State University of New York Press.

Glasser, W. (1992). *The quality school: Managing students without coercion* (2nd ed.). New York: Harper.

Gordon, D.T. (Ed.). (2003). *A nation reformed? American education 20 years after* A Nation at Risk. Cambridge, MA: Harvard University Press.

Hallinger, P., & McCary, C.E. (1990). Developing the strategic thinking of instructional leaders. *Elementary School Journal, 91*(2), 89–108.

Hallowell, E.M. (1999). *Connect: 12 vital ties that open your heart, lengthen your life, and deepen your soul.* New York: Pocket.

Hargreaves, A. (1994). *Changing teachers, changing times: Teachers' work and culture in the postmodern age.* New York: Teachers College Press.

Harste, J.C., & Burke, C.L. (1977). A new hypothesis for reading teacher research: Both the *teaching* and *learning* of reading are theoretically based. In P.D. Pearson (Ed.), *Reading: Theory, research, and practice* (26th yearbook of the National Reading Conference, pp. 32–40). Clemson, SC: National Reading Conference.

Hendricks-Lee, M.S., Soled, S.W., & Yinger, R.J. (1995). Sustaining reform through teacher learning. *Language Arts, 72*(4), 288–292.

Hord, S.M. (1987). *Taking charge of change.* Alexandria, VA: Association for Supervision and Curriculum Development.

Horton, M., & Freire, P. (with Bell, B., Gaventa, J., & Peters, J.M., Eds.). (1990). *We make the road by walking: Conversations on education and social change.* Philadelphia: Temple University Press.

Hubbard, R., & Power, B.M. (1993). *The art of classroom inquiry: A handbook for teacher-researchers.* Portsmouth, NH: Heinemann.

Huberman, A.M., & Miles, M.B. (1986). Rethinking the quest for school improvement: Some findings from the DESSI study. In A. Lieberman (Ed.), *Rethinking school improvement: Research, craft, and concept* (pp. 61–81). New York: Teachers College Press.

International Listening Association. Homepage. Retrieved May 18, 2004, from http://www.listen.org.

Joyce, B., Murphy, C., Showers, B., & Murphy, J. (1989). School renewal as cultural change. *Educational Leadership, 47*(3), 70–77.

Joyce, B., & Showers, B. (1988). *Student achievement through staff development.* New York: Longman.

Killion, J. (2003). Use these 6 keys to open doors to literacy. *Journal of Staff Development, 24*(2), 10–16.

Kohn, A. (1999). *Punished by rewards: The trouble with gold stars, incentive plans, A's, praise and other bribes.* Boston: Houghton-Mifflin.

Lapp, D., Fisher, D., Flood, J., & Frey, N. (2003). Dual role of the urban reading specialist. *Journal of Staff Development, 24*(2), 33–35.

Lawrence-Lightfoot, S. (1999). *Respect: An exploration.* Reading, MA: Perseus.

Le Fevre, D., & Richardson, V. (2002). Staff development in early reading intervention programs: The facilitator. *Teaching and Teacher Education, 18*(4), 483–500.

Levine, D., Lowe, R., Peterson, B., & Tenorio, R. (Eds.). (1995). *Rethinking schools: An agenda for change.* New York: New Press.

Lieberman, A., & Miller, L. (1999). *Teachers transforming their world and their work.* New York: Teachers College Press.

Little, J.W. (1987). Teachers as colleagues. In V. Richardson (Ed.), *Educators' handbook: A research perspective* (pp. 503–525). New York: Longman.

Little, J.W. (1990). The persistence of privacy: Autonomy and initiative in teachers' professional relations. *Teachers College Record, 91*(4), 509–536.

Lyons, C. (2002). Becoming an effective literacy coach: What does it take? In E.M. Rodgers & G.S. Pinnell (Eds.), *Learning from teaching in literacy education: New perspectives on professional development* (pp. 93–118). Portsmouth, NH: Heinemann.

Lyons, C.A., & Pinnell, G.S. (2001). *Systems for change in literacy education: A guide to professional development*. Portsmouth, NH: Heinemann.

MacLean, P.D. (1990). *The triune brain in evolution: Role in paleocerebral functions*. New York: Plenum.

Marzano, R.J. (1992). *A different kind of classroom: Teaching with dimensions of learning*. Alexandria, VA: Association for Supervision and Curriculum Development.

McClain, G., & Romaine, D.S. (2002). *The everything managing people book: Quick and easy ways to build, motivate, and nurture a first-rate team*. Avon, MA: Adams Media.

Meyer, R.J. (1998). *Composing a teacher study group: Learning about inquiry in primary classrooms*. Mahwah, NJ: Erlbaum.

National Center for Education Statistics. (2003). *Schools and staffing survey: 2003–2004*. Washington, DC: U.S. Department of Education.

National Commission on Excellence in Education. (1983). *A nation at risk: The imperative for educational reform*. Washington, DC: U.S. Department of Education.

National Council of Teachers of English. (2000). *NCTE reading initiative overview*. Retrieved August 2, 2004, from www/ncte.org/profdev/onsite/readinit

National Council of Teachers of Mathematics. (1989). *Curriculum and evaluation standards for school mathematics*. Reston, VA: Author.

National Institute of Child Health and Human Development. (2000). *Report of the National Reading Panel. Teaching children to read: An evidence-based assessment of the scientific research literature on reading and its implications for reading instruction* (NIH Publication No. 00-4769). Washington, DC: U.S. Government Printing Office.

Nichols, M.P. (1995). *The lost art of listening: How learning to listen can improve relationships*. New York: Guilford.

Norton, J. (2001). A storybook breakthrough. *Journal of Staff Development, 22*(5), 22–25.

Palmer, P.J. (1998). *The courage to teach: Exploring the inner landscape of a teacher's life*. San Francisco: Jossey-Bass.

Perrone, V. (Ed.). (1991). *Expanding student assessment*. Alexandria, VA: Association for Supervision and Curriculum Development.

Peterson, K.D. (1988). Mechanisms of culture building and principals' work. *Education and Urban Society, 20*(3), 250–261.

Phillips, D.C. (Ed.). (2000). *Constructivism in education: Opinions and second opinions on controversial issues*. Chicago: National Society for the Study of Education.

Rhodes, L.K., & Shanklin, N. (1993). *Windows into literacy: Assessing learners K–8*. Portsmouth, NH: Heinemann.

Ross, J.A., & Regan, E.M. (1993). Sharing professional experience: Its impact on professional development. *Teaching & Teacher Education, 9*(1), 91–106.

Routman, R. (1994). *Invitations: Changing as teachers and learners, K–12*. Portsmouth, NH: Heinemann.

Sandholtz, K. (2002). *Beyond juggling: Rebalancing your busy life*. Berkeley, CA: Berrett-Koehler.

Sarason, S.B. (1996). *Revisiting "The culture of the school and the problem of change"*. New York: Teachers College Press.

Sarason, S.B., & Lorentz, E.M. (1998). *Crossing boundaries: Collaboration, coordination, and the redefinition of resources*. San Francisco: Jossey-Bass.

Schlechty, P.C. (1990). *Schools for the 21st century: Leadership imperatives for educational reform*. San Francisco: Jossey-Bass.

Schlechty, P.C. (1992). *Creating schools for the 21st century: Practical guidelines for achieving systemwide change on a day-to-day basis*. San Francisco: Jossey-Bass.

Schön, D.A. (1987). *Educating the reflective practitioner: Toward a new design for teaching and learning in the professions*. San Francisco: Jossey-Bass.

Sergiovanni, T.J. (1992). *Moral leadership: Getting to the heart of school improvement.* San Francisco: Jossey-Bass.

Shanahan, T. (2003). Research-based reading instruction: Myths about the National Reading Panel Report. *The Reading Teacher, 56,* 646–655.

Shannon, P. (1998). *Reading poverty.* Portsmouth, NH: Heinemann.

Short, K.G., Harste, J.C., & Burke, C. (1996). *Creating classrooms for authors and inquirers* (2nd ed.). Portsmouth, NH: Heinemann.

Short, K., Kaufman, G., Kaser, S., Kahn, L.H., & Crawford, K.M. (1999). "Teacher-watching": Examining teacher talk in literature circles. *Language Arts, 76*(5), 377–385.

Showers, B. (1985). Teachers coaching teachers. *Educational Leadership, 42*(7), 43–48.

Showers, B., & Joyce, B. (1996). The evolution of peer coaching. *Educational Leadership, 53*(6), 12–16.

Sizer, T.R. (1992). *Horace's school: Redesigning the American high school.* Boston: Houghton Mifflin.

Spring, J.H. (2002). *Political agendas for education: From the religious right to the Green Party* (2nd ed.). Mahwah, NJ: Erlbaum.

Stallings, J.A. (1981). *Testing teachers' in-class instruction and measuring change resulting from staff development.* Mountain View, CA: Teaching and Learning Institute. (ERIC Document Reproduction Service No. ED 241 545)

Stokes, L. (2001). Lessons from an inquiring school: Forms of inquiry and conditions for teacher learning. In A. Lieberman & L. Miller (Eds.), *Teachers caught in the action: Professional development that matters* (pp. 141–158). New York: Teachers College Press.

Stone, D., Patton, B., & Heen, S. (1999). *Difficult conversations: How to discuss what matters most.* New York: Viking.

Sturtevant, E.G. (2003). *The literacy coach: A key to improving teaching and learning in secondary schools.* Washington, DC: Alliance for Excellent Education.

Swartz, S., Shook, R., & Klein, A. (2001). *Foundation for California Early Literacy Learning: CELL, ExLL, and Second Chance.* Redlands, CA: Foundation for California Early Literacy Learning. (ERIC Document Reproduction Service No. ED 452 510)

Sweeney, D. (2003). *Learning along the way: Professional development by and for teachers.* Portland, ME: Stenhouse.

Sweeney, D.R., & Harris, L.S. (2002). Learning to work with—not against—a system. *Journal of Staff Development, 23*(3), 16–19.

Taberski, S. (2000). *On solid ground: Strategies for teaching reading K–3.* Portsmouth, NH: Heinemann.

Tannen, D. (1986). *That's not what I mean! How conversational style makes or breaks relationships.* New York: Ballantine.

Tannen, D. (1994). *Talking from 9 to 5: How women's and men's conversational styles affect who gets heard, who gets credit, and what gets done at work.* New York: Morrow.

Tierney, R.J., & Zalokar, B. (2003). *Interactive assessment: Teachers, parents, and students as partners.* Norwood, MA: Christopher-Gordon.

Tyack, D.B., & Cuban, L. (1995). *Tinkering toward utopia: A century of public school reform.* Cambridge, MA: Harvard University Press.

Tye, K.A., & Tye, B.B. (1984). Teacher isolation and school reform. *Phi Delta Kappan, 65,* 319–322.

Vogt, M., & Shearer, B.A. (2003). *Reading specialists in the real world: A sociocultural view.* Boston: Allyn & Bacon.

Wheatley, M.J., & Kellner-Rogers, M. (1996). *A simpler way.* San Francisco: Barrett-Koehler.

Zebrowitz, L.A. (1997). *Reading faces: Window to the soul?* Boulder, CO: Westview.

Zeichner, K.M., & Liston, D.P. (1996). *Reflective teaching: An introduction.* Mahwah, NJ: Erlbaum.

INDEX

References followed by *t* or *f* indicate tables or figures, respectively.

BUDDY READING STATION, 48
BURKE, C., 99, 153

C

CARNAHAN, D., 164

CARR, W., 164

CBAM. *See* Concerns-Based Adoption Model (CBAM)

CENTERED FEELING, 133–134

CHANDLER, K., 157

CHANGE, 6; Buddhist concepts of, 158; changing educators' understanding of, 26–34; effects of, 153; experts' opinions of, 155–158; focus of, 17–23, 156–158; methods of, 31–32; overview of, 14–15; past focus of, 15; resistance to, 27–28; stereotypes of, 25; technologies of, 15–17, 155–156; telling teacher to, 127

CHANGING TEACHERS, CHANGING TIMES (HARGREAVES), 157

CHOICE THEORY, 156

CLASSROOM DEMONSTRATIONS: debriefing session for, 128; in early part of school year, 46–47; teachers' comfort level with, 127–128

COACHING, 3. *See also* literacy coaching

COACHING: EVOKING EXCELLENCE IN OTHERS (FLAHERTY), 157

COACHING SUCCESSFULLY (EATON & JOHNSON), 130

COCHRAN-SMITH, M., 158

COGNITION, 20, 157

COGNITIVE COACHING (COSTA & GARMSTON), 157

COGNITIVE DISSONANCE, 20

COHEN, S.S., 164

COLLABORATION. *See* literacy coaching

COMMUNICATION: to address poor goals, 115*f*; overview of, 62; resources for, 161–162, 163–164; tips for eliciting, 67–72; western society's assumptions of, 84. *See also specific types*

COMMUNICATIVE DIALOGUE, 84

COMMUNITY, DIVERSITY, AND CONFLICT AMONG SCHOOLTEACHERS (ACHINSTEIN), 163

CONCERNS-BASED ADOPTION MODEL (CBAM), 19, 157

CONNECT (HALLOWELL), 164, 166

CONSISTENCY, 49

CONSORTIUM OF READING EXCELLENCE (CORE), 9

CONTRIVED COLLEGIALITY, 163

CORRIE, L., 163

COSTA, A.L., 156, 157

THE COURAGE TO TEACH (PALMER), 168

CRAWFORD, K.M., 99

CREATING SCHOOLS FOR THE 21ST CENTURY (SCHLECHTY), 157–158

CUBAN, L., 6, 29, 153

CULTURE. *See* school culture

D

DATA: analyses of, 104–106; types of, 162

DATA COLLECTION, 21; in inquiry groups, 101, 104; for monitoring success, 94*t*; in role of literacy coach, 138

NORTON, J., 8

NOTE-TAKING: in individual conferences, 78; as listening strategy, 64; in team
    meetings, 95, 96, 97f

NOTHING SPECIAL (BECK), 158

O

OBSERVATION, 141–142, 167

ON SOLID GROUND (TABERSKI), 158

OPEN-ENDED QUESTIONS, 105, 137

OPEN-MINDED PERSPECTIVE, 109

P

PALMER, P.J., 168

PARAPHRASING, 64

PARENTS, 47–48, 159

PARTICIPATION LEVELS, 85

PATTON, B., 163, 164, 165

PEER COACHING, 3–4, 141–142, 167

PERFORMANCE REVIEW, 140

PERRONE, V., 156

PETERSON, K.D., 152, 155

PHILLIPS, D.C., 154

PINNELL, G.S., 8, 158, 166

PLANNING, 77–78

POLICYMAKERS, 29

POLITICAL AGENDAS FOR EDUCATION (SPRING), 155

POLITICS, 155

POWER, B.M., 20–21, 104, 157

POWER STRUGGLES, 55–56

PRINCIPALS: discussing change with, 32–33; first meeting with, 39; and focus of
    school reform, 17; test score focus of, 126–127

PROBLEM SOLVING: in context of team meetings, 91–95; letting go of, 134–135;
    myths about, 71; questions to elicit, 69–70

PROCESS, 20–21, 89

PROFESSIONAL DEVELOPMENT WORKSHOPS, 128, 166

PULL-OUT PROGRAM, 127, 143–144

PUNISHED BY REWARDS (KOHN), 156–157

PUNISHMENTS, 19, 113

PUT-DOWNS, 90, 129

PUT-ON-THE-BRAKES GROUP, 40, 42, 42t

Q–R

QUESTIONS: to elicit teachers' problem solving, 69–70; index of, 146–151; and
    respect, 58, 59t; in role of literacy coach, 137; to steer individual conferences,
    76; for surveys, 105

RACIST STATEMENTS, 90, 129